TAROT
FOR BEGINNERS

TAROT
FOR BEGINNERS

TERI SCHURE

Copyright © 2024 by Teri Schure

All rights reserved. No part of this publication may be reproduced, in whole or in part, stored in a retrieval system, or transmitted in any form by any means—electronic, mechanical, photocopying, recording, or other—without written permission from the author.

For permission or further contact information, write to:
Teri Schure, All Media, Inc., 124 Grove Avenue,
#401, Cedarhurst, NY 11516.

Cover & layout design:
www.kimmontefortebookdesign.com

Cover image credit: Nikita Filippov

ISBN: 978-1-7352214-2-7 (PB)
ISBN: 978-1-7352214-3-4 (EB)
Library of Congress Control
Number: 2024908389

Printed in the United States of America
10 9 8 7 6 5 4 3 2 1

DEDICATION

In the late 1970s, a close friend and work colleague turned me on to Tarot cards, but it wasn't until March 2020, during the Covid lockdown, that I bought a deck for myself.

Four years later, I feel as though I can finally read the cards reasonably well, but I still refer to my notes—this book—for guidance.

Tarot for Beginners is dedicated to my friend and hero, Leslie Jacobs, who taught me way more than Tarot and is one of the kindest, most courageous, positive, and resilient women I have ever known.

TABLE OF CONTENTS

Tarot 101   1

The Major Arcana Cards Explained.   2

The Major Arcana Cards   3–24

The Court Cards Explained.   25

The Minor Arcana Cards Explained   26

Wands   27–41

Cups.   42–56

Swords   57–71

Pentacles   72–86

SIGNS OF THE ZODIAC

ARIES: March 21–April 19

TAURUS: April 20–May 20

GEMINI: May 21–June 20

CANCER: June 21–July 22

LEO: July 23–August 22

VIRGO: August 23–September 22

LIBRA: September 23–October 22

SCORPIO: October 23–November 21

SAGITTARIUS: November 22–December 21

CAPRICORN: December 22–January 19

AQUARIUS: January 20–February 18

PISCES: February 19–March 20

TAROT 101

The elite played tarot cards in the 1400s as a parlor game—a divination or occult connection only became popular in the late 1500s. In England, in 1889, Arthur Edward Waite, a spiritual seeker and mystic, wrote one of the first books about how to read tarot, ultimately creating the world's most influential deck of tarot cards: The Rider-Waite® Tarot Deck.

Waite was a member of the secret society called the Hermetic Order of the Golden Dawn. In 1909, Waite paid Pamela Colman Smith, a fellow Golden Dawn member, a flat fee to illustrate his tarot deck. Smith was a Black woman of Jamaican descent, born in London to American parents, and studied art at the Pratt Institute in New York. Rider Publishing put their name on the deck but never gave credit to the incredibly talented Ms. Smith—nor did she or her family ever benefit financially from the Rider-Waite tarot cards.

The Rider-Waite cards have greatly helped me facilitate a free-association approach to tarot reading, primarily due to Ms. Smith's creative genius. For this reason, I used the Rider-Waite tarot cards to write my book, so you will need to buy their deck if you want to use my interpretation of the deck's imagery.

The easiest way to begin a tarot reading is with one card. Once you familiarize yourself with the images and stories behind each card, step up to a three-card reading. Many readers use past, present, and future, but I prefer to read the cards without placing a time frame on them. You're the tarot reader, so you do you. Just remember, practice makes perfect. Let the cards do the talking—the pictures will guide you through the reading.

In a three-card reading, I ask the querent (the person I'm reading) to shuffle and lay out three cards face down in a row. Only the querent should touch the cards. The querent will lay the cards face down, then turn them over face up, precisely as they placed them.

The reading of the cards, upright or upside down (reversed), is from the position and perspective of the reader. Reversed tarot cards may represent the excessive energy of a card and are not necessarily the opposite of an upright card.

I also like to keep a notebook of my past readings so I can go back and review the cards, which often offers additional insight into them.

THE MAJOR ARCANA CARDS EXPLAINED

Arcana is derived from the Latin word *"arcanus,"* which means "secret." The Major Arcana cards symbolize the karmic influences, lessons learned, and the spiritual journey that impacts your life and your soul's path to enlightenment.

These cards are often considered the most influential and powerful cards in the deck and play a crucial role in interpreting the overall long-term aspects of a tarot reading.

The significance of the Major Arcana cards is complex and profound, creating a storyline of the querent's triumphs, failures, struggles, regrets, self-discovery, and personal growth.

Pulling Major Arcana cards in a tarot reading signifies the need to face head-on the trials and tribulations you may be facing in your life and often serves as the anchor for the reading.

The rest of the cards in the reading will usually connect to the central message and meaning of the Major Arcana.

If the Major Arcana cards make up most of your reading, you may soon embark on a life-changing situation that could upend your life's trajectory.

If most of the Major Arcana cards are reversed, it may indicate that you need to open your eyes to the reality of what's happening around you before moving forward. Whenever the Major Arcana is part of a reading, it acts as the framework and helps to reinforce, guide, and connect the message and pattern of all the pulled cards.

The Major Arcana, often called Triumph or Trump Cards, total 22, from the Fool at zero to the World at 21. They are frequently referred to as 22 doors or 22 pivotal moments in human and spiritual development and are used to explore one's psyche, consciousness, and mental state.

When you draw a Major Arcana card, take it seriously because the message may be crucial to the overall reading.

THE FOOL (0)

Keyword: **Causality**

The Fool bears the number zero, which signifies unlimited potential, and he is the central character in the Major Arcana cards. According to the ancient fortune tellers, he travels through all the Major Arcana cards on his quest to find himself or his purpose. His travels through each Major Arcana card provide insight into life's meaning. His life's journey ends with The World card (21). The Fool is a stand-in for the self as we progress down life's many roads.

The Fool is so preoccupied with dreams, visions, wonderment, and excitement that he might not see the cliff ahead of him. At his heel is a dog, perhaps warning him to stop and think about his choices. He probably has all he needs in the small bag on his staff to do or be anything he wants. He only has to stop and unpack.

The Fool reminds us that there are ripple effects for everything we do and everything we don't do. Ask yourself what the ripple effects of your actions are.

The Fool may also signify some sort of Fool's Journey. Don't be a fool or fooled by someone near and dear. Don't just jump; think before acting, and watch your step.

You may be on your way to a new beginning, job, home, or relationship. Something new is about to happen, but tread carefully. The Fool denotes fresh beginnings, but take care that your actions don't get you into trouble. Be careful not to overindulge, and watch your spending.

REVERSED

Don't be easily manipulated, and stay away from manipulative people. Be careful of recklessness, vanity, inconsideration, and mania. Don't make hasty decisions.

Be wary of wicked fools and people who are careless, neglectful, or emotionally absent. Don't accept indifference: take a stand against foolishness and foolish behavior. The Fool card, in reverse, warns of intoxication, delirium, frenzy, and betrayal.

THE MAGICIAN (1)

Keyword: **Transformation**

The Magician is number one—*numero uno*. He has everything he needs to succeed, but he is the only one who can make the magic happen. He has an infinity symbol over his head, representing limitlessness. One arm points up while the other points down, perhaps depicting the ups and downs of life. All four suits are on the table. The Magician wears a belt adorned with a serpent swallowing its tail, symbolizing the cycle of life and death.

If the querent is male, this card is about him. If the querent is female, this is not a lover, but someone else—someone neutral. The Magician is a determined, talented, and competent leader. Don't underestimate him.

He is surrounded by the rose of Sharon, a hardy shrub that can survive many adverse conditions—poor soil, heat, humidity, drought, and air pollution—yet it still flourishes and thrives.

The lilies of the valley are above and below him, symbolizing rebirth, serenity, and a new beginning. A favorite of brides, they may represent innocence, motherhood, and purity and are believed to bring prosperity, love, and continued happiness. But they can also symbolize sadness and are often placed on graves or in funeral floral arrangements to honor a death.

The Magician wants you to tackle any illnesses head-on and not be afraid to address pain, loss, and disaster. Self-confidence and strength are crucial to achieving long-term health, happiness, and contentment.

REVERSED

The Magician, in reverse, might suggest that there is mental illness around you. Have you recently experienced an embarrassment or disgrace? Has someone been harassing you? The Magician, in reverse, suggests manipulation, confusion, and dishonesty.

The card in reverse tells you to tap into your full potential—don't hold yourself back because transformational change may be in your near future. Only you have the power to change things up.

THE HIGH PRIESTESS (2)

Keyword: **Instinctive**

The High Priestess sits in front of a hanging banner decorated with pomegranates, symbolizing abundance, fertility, and femininity. Two pillars are on either side of the High Priestess, creating an entrance to her space. She sits between the pillars, possibly indicating the equality and balance she strives for. One pillar is black with the letter B, and the other is white with the letter J. Perhaps those letters are significant to you.

The black and white colors of the pillars symbolize a contrast or dichotomy—perhaps masculine versus feminine, darkness versus light, war versus peace, or her two states of mind: the conscious (aware) versus the subconscious (unaware).

The High Priestess wears a stunning blue robe, and a large cross adorns her chest. She wears a horned crown, symbolizing her knowledge and respected status. She holds a scroll in her lap engraved with the letters spelling out TORA. Her robe partially covers the scroll, hinting there may be more letters. Perhaps the word is Torah—Jewish versus Christian?

The crescent moon below her symbolizes her connection with the daily cycle of life, although a waning crescent may indicate the end of something.

If the querent is male, this is a woman who interests him, not necessarily his lover. If the querent is a woman, this, in all likelihood, represents her. The High Priestess looks pensive. Perhaps you are holding on to someone or something that you should let go of.

REVERSED

The reversed High Priestess warns of repressed emotions, someone confused about her purpose or unable to move past something. Don't be afraid to move forward.

Be wary of those who profess to have your back; their intentions might not be genuine.

The High Priestess wants you to turn inward. Meditate, journal, make art, or do anything that gets you in touch with that part of you that's difficult to access consciously.

THE EMPRESS (3)

Keyword: **Motherly**

The Empress is the matriarch of all the tarot mothers and appears in the card as a beautiful woman with a peaceful aura. She wears a magnificent crown of 12 stars, representing her connection with the number 12. In numerology, 12 represents harmony and balance and is often associated with tolerance, effective communication, imagination, creativity, beauty, grace, cooperation, optimism, self-sufficiency, and self-determination. Ask yourself: Who is this person to you?

Sometimes, the Empress is a stand-in for your mother, a maternal figure in your life, or the mother of your children. In a more general sense, the Empress urges you to live and love passionately, kindly, and with unconstrained feelings.

Her robe is adorned with pomegranates, the symbol of fertility, and she sits upon a luxurious array of cushions and flowing red velvet. Next to her throne is a cushion bearing the symbol of Venus, the planet of love. A lush forest and winding stream surround the Empress, signifying her connection with Mother Nature. The towering trees and the pooling water near her feet indicate her sense of peace and loving disposition. In front of her, golden wheat springs from the soil, reflecting recent abundance.

The Empress is a nurturer. She represents gentleness, a connection to nature, and motherly or romantic love. Whether we regard her as a mother, a lover, or a connection to nature, there is one common thread: a whole-hearted, honest, and straightforward approach to life. The Empress symbolizes fertility, motherhood, pregnancy, and fruitfulness. She is multidimensional and will unequivocally support you, no matter what. But she can also signify long days ahead. Are you having some difficulty or doubts about something? Don't be afraid of the unknown, and don't be ignorant of what is right in front of you.

REVERSED

In reverse, the Empress cautions not to overly depend on someone or something. There is an emptiness, a vacillation, and a suffocation surrounding you or someone you know. To reveal the problem, you will need to unravel it.

THE EMPEROR (4)

Keyword: **Fatherly**

The Emperor is the patriarch of all the tarot fathers. He can be a boss, a partner, a father, or a father figure. The Emperor sits on a large stone throne adorned with four ram heads, a possible connection to Aries (March 21–April 19). In his right hand, he holds an ankh, the Egyptian symbol of life, and in his left hand, an orb, representing spiritual protection or guidance. Perhaps a spirit is trying to come through to you.

The Emperor wears a red robe, indicating his passion, survival, and love of life. Underneath his robe, he wears a suit of armor, symbolizing his role as protector. Conflict doesn't intimidate him, and he won't hesitate to protect those he cares about. His long white beard symbolizes his wisdom and years of experience. His gold crown serves as a reminder that he is someone who knows what he's talking about, so you should pay attention to what he has to say.

Behind his throne lies a looming range of mountains, signifying that a solid foundation backs him. Beneath the mountain on the left side flows a tiny bit of water, perhaps suggesting that his exterior might be tough, but he has an emotional side. It takes time for him to open up, but his soft side will be revealed once he trusts you. He is adept at finding the calm in the chaos. He knows what he wants but will never break the rules to achieve his goal.

REVERSED

The Emperor, in reverse, signifies rigidity, domination, immaturity, and possible abuse of power. Perhaps you're holding back from speaking your mind because you fear your truth will cause strife and retribution if you say too much. You might consider using other channels to speak your mind, like journaling or writing a letter.

If you're single, search for someone who will offer a stable foundation for the future. But beware. This person may be someone who can provide for you but don't lose your light or independence. Ask yourself if your relationship is causing you anxiety or unhappiness. Perhaps your significant other has become overbearing, possessive, and dominating, putting enormous strain on the relationship and making it almost impossible for the two of you to get along.

THE HIEROPHANT (5)

Keyword: **Counsel**

The Hierophant often aligns with Taurus (April 20–May 20). He is seated on a throne between two pillars, symbolizing two sides of a situation. He wears a triple crown, and crosses adorn his robe and shoes. The two crossed keys at his feet bear the number eight, a symbol of balance. The keys may also symbolize something that's being kept locked away.

Below him are two men, perhaps seeking spiritual guidance. When the Hierophant card is pulled, it may represent someone you have relied on to help in a difficult situation. The Hierophant can also suggest a religious conflict, or you may be seeking a deeper meaning in your life.

Perhaps the card asks you to accept people from other backgrounds, cultures, and religions. We learn the most about others through interaction with them. An uncompromising stance on something can cause others to question your sincerity.

We tend to stay stuck in our attitudes and beliefs because it's what we know and helps us feel safe. Now might be the time to do some soul-searching and make a change.

REVERSED

In reverse, the Hierophant suggests you are conflicted regarding an authoritative figure or religious belief. A new approach to something causing division in your life may be necessary.

There may be unrest or rebellion, causing you to question your belief in something. Or perhaps a relationship breakdown, poor counsel, a rejection of family values, or a friendship issue is weighing on you.

If this is the case, try to make a peace pact without showing weakness. Be kind but firm, and don't rush to judgment, religious or otherwise. Be mindful of hurting others with your words and understand situations and challenges before you offer an opinion. And stay away from stereotyping.

THE LOVERS (6)

Keyword: **Harmony**

Two naked figures stand tall in a lush garden, signifying Adam and Eve in the Garden of Eden. Behind Eve is an apple tree with a snake ready to strike at her head. Above them is a winged angel, her arms outstretched to protect them.

While many interpret the Lovers card as purely about romantic and sexual love, many types of love exist. The Lovers card can be about any relationship in which love is felt intensely and deeply.

The Lovers card can represent the duality surrounding who you want to be and who you want to be with. It often symbolizes choosing between what you desire and what you know would be better for you in the long term. It also suggests that who you want to spend the rest of your life with might not be the right question. Instead, try asking yourself who you can't live without. The Lovers card also signifies symmetry, partnerships, unity, attraction, love, and beauty.

REVERSED

Are you experiencing an imbalance, discord, or disharmony in some capacity? Are you or someone else disloyal, jealous, overly possessive, or overprotective? Beware the temptations of the heart.

Or maybe a rift is developing in the relationship. Try not to overthink things. Don't make hasty decisions, and watch your tongue; once your words are out there, you can't shove them back in. Above all, resist the urge to give up. If at first you don't succeed, try, try again.

Relationship-wise, you may need to come to terms with whatever arguments or problems you two may be experiencing. The best way to understand each other is to talk it out. But you also need to be strong enough to accept that you can't make someone love you. As long as you try your best, that's all you can do. Know when to walk away, and do it with dignity and with your head held high.

THE CHARIOT (7)

Keyword: **Resilience**

The Chariot is often linked to the Cancer zodiac sign (June 21–July 22) and signifies control, resilience, and triumph over the tough stuff. The Chariot can also suggest assistance and support in times of distress. The card depicts a figure inside a vehicle pulled by two sphinxes, one black and one white, symbolizing opposing forces. The charioteer's task is to guide these sphinxes toward a common goal. He sits below a blue canopy of white stars and wears two crescent moons on his shoulders, representing the spiritual influence guiding him. Perhaps he's a spirit coming through with a message for you.

The Chariot suggests you use your willpower, determination, and grit to remain committed to your choice if you're in a quandary about something. Try not to resist change; it might be the best thing for you in the long term.

The Chariot tarot card alludes to overcoming challenges and gaining victory by maintaining control of your surroundings. The Chariot's message reminds you to never give up on your dreams and goals. But you must maintain focus, confidence, and determination as you wind through life's twists, turns, and detours. The Chariot urges you to take control of your love life: with confidence and courage, you will reap the benefits of your efforts. Balance is the key. Is your relationship suffering because you or someone else is a workaholic or spending too much time away from home?

REVERSED

The Chariot, in reverse, can depict litigation, quarrels, and lack of direction. You may need to rein in your impulses, especially regarding your spending. You may be at the mercy of an opposing force and unable or unwilling to muster the strength to put your foot down. Maybe you're taking everything lying down, and life seems to be dragging you in any direction it pleases. Try your best to be in control of your life. Let this be a wake-up call and reminder that you need to take charge of your destiny and do it soon. If things are out of balance, give yourself a pep talk, pull on your armor, and accelerate full throttle. Don't feel confident? Fake it until you do. As long as you're acting with kindness, determination, and balance, you will surely succeed.

STRENGTH (8)

Keyword: **Persistence**

The Strength card represents the ability to stay calm and overcome challenging situations and may connect to Leo (July 23–August 22). The woman gently strokes a lion on its forehead and under its jaw. The docile lion looks up at her lovingly—he feels comfortable with the woman. His tail is between his legs, a sign of submission. Her dominance over the lion signifies that she has courage and compassion, but she's in control. She's gentle with him and has tamed him with her calming, loving energy. She has boundless affection for the lion and all his wild tendencies. She defines the word "lionhearted."

The lion symbolizes desire, passion, and power, and in taming him, the woman shows that animal instinct and power can be expressed positively when inner strength and resilience are applied. Her white robe represents the purity of her spirit and intent. Her flowered belt and crown represent her love of nature. Above her head is an infinity symbol, representing her persistence and infinite potential, meaning she has time. This woman uses a gentle approach and a compassionate heart to overcome her obstacles. Treat yourself with the same compassion and kindness that you extend to others. This card may also suggest the need to rein in a bad boy or wild girl. The Strength card asks you to persist in your endeavors and not lose hope but know when to give up.

REVERSED

The Strength card, in reverse, suggests the need to tame your emotions, or perhaps someone in your life has passive-aggressive tendencies. It also represents insecurity, weakness, doubt, disbelief, and fear. If you're avoiding a situation you feel you can't control, your resilience is needed now more than ever. Resist the urge to run away. Summon your courage and face the problem head-on. The longer you let things loom over you, the more ferocious the "lion" grows. While inaction is a protective mechanism, don't let others rule your life. Face your fears and tame them. Examine the people around you: is someone making you feel small or holding you back? Maybe you're a combination of wild and docile. Perhaps it's time to take an honest look at yourself. Who do you see, and do you need to tame or rein in some of your actions? Recognize and accept who you are—use your resilience to face your obstacles and know that you're lion-strong.

THE HERMIT (9)

Keyword: **Solitary**

When the Hermit appears in a reading, it signifies that, while our goals can be attained, the journey may not be smooth or easy. Perhaps you've been forced to struggle through hardships along the way. It may also suggest the need for a spiritual journey of some sort. Whatever happens, you need to open up to others and not get too comfortable in solitude.

The Hermit stands alone on a snowy mountaintop, holding a lit lantern. In tarot, the night represents the unknown. The lantern is his inner guiding light. The six-pointed star within the lantern symbolizes reincarnation, communication with spirits, or a soul from the afterlife. It could also signify the Star of David or a connection to the number six.

The mountain peak the Hermit is standing on represents a feeling of isolation despite achievement and growth. Beneath his feet lie the pain and difficulties he has endured to reach the top. Perhaps the Hermit has struggled through hardships along life's journey.

The Hermit signifies truth-seeking, introspection, contemplation, guidance, self-discovery, and spiritual understanding. Don't become detached or separated from others. That will only cause more emptiness. Try to get out more and avoid turning inward. Use your intuition and stop keeping secrets. Stop concealing your thoughts and feelings and speak your truth. You're a force to be reckoned with, but you need to believe in yourself. Let your inner voice be a lantern to guide you through the night.

REVERSED

The Hermit, in reverse, signifies fear, isolation, seclusion, loneliness, depression, discouragement, and anxiety. You may be overly cautious about something, which might be the best approach. Tread carefully because someone may be concealing something or disguising the true purpose behind their relationship with you. Put yourself out there, but use prudence and caution. Someone you trust may be disloyal, dishonest, unprincipled, or corrupt, so keep your eyes open, be aware, and most importantly, be careful.

WHEEL OF FORTUNE (10)

Keyword: **Destiny**

The Wheel of Fortune is one of the most symbolic cards in tarot; full of symbols and hidden meanings, like the sphinx (strength), snake (life force), and Anubis (underworld). There are four winged creatures in each card corner, associated with four zodiac signs: the angel is Aquarius (January 20–February 18), the eagle is Scorpio (October 23–November 21), the lion is Leo (July 23–August 22), and the bull is Taurus (April 20–May 20). Each creature holds a book representing wisdom; their wings might signify that spirits are present.

The wheel contains three Hebrew letters—*heh* (breath), *yod* (fate), and *vav* (thorn), possibly signifying someone Jewish or something related to Judaism.

Some look at the A and O as blood types, blood disorders, or the first letters of people in your life—and then there are the letters R and T. In the center of the wheel are the symbols of the building blocks of life: mercury (spirit), sulfur (soul), water (life), and salt (longevity). Without all four, we would cease to exist.

The circle signifies a cyclical process, destiny, karma, fate, or a turning point. Don't be afraid to take chances. The Wheel of Fortune keeps turning; you can do nothing about it. It's the circle of life, and you need to make peace with its impermanence.

REVERSED

The Wheel of Fortune, in reverse, suggests that someone is unnecessarily and unfairly hurting you. Think honestly about your current life situation and who may be causing you anxiety, and try to avoid them or speak your mind if you can't. If things are going great for you, know it won't last forever. If life is difficult, don't worry because it will get better—this, too, shall pass. You may be facing misfortune, or you may have lost control of something. Try not to be overly despondent at what appears to be too many mishaps or unforeseen setbacks. And don't be resistant to change. It might be time to move on. You might need to walk away from negativity to change your trajectory—all things can be reversed. Your destiny is not predetermined. Consider proactively taking charge of your life and pay close attention to the actions of those around you.

JUSTICE (11)

Keyword: **Balance**

The Justice card represents fairness, strong moral principles, honesty, and decency. It suggests you are responsible for knowing right from wrong and living a fair and balanced life. The figure of Justice sits in front of a loosely hung purple curtain, signifying compassion. She sits between two stone pillars, a symbol of balance. She holds a sword in her right hand, showing the necessity to be fair but also forceful. The sword points upwards, denoting a firm and final decision. The double-edged blade is a reminder that our actions always carry consequences. The evenly balanced scales in her left hand suggest the importance of balance and symbolize her impartiality.

The Justice card is about seeking the truth and determining right from wrong. If you're about to make an important decision, the Justice card indicates that you need to weigh the facts of the different sides of the situation and come to a fair and objective conclusion. The Justice card stands for clarity, truthfulness, transparency, and accuracy. Do the right thing and be the better person.

When the Justice card is pulled, it may be time to make hard choices and make your decisions honestly and fairly. Perhaps you have wronged someone, or someone you know has wronged you. Either way, you should know that whoever was behind the wrongdoing will not escape justice—including you. The Justice card can symbolize a conceptual or abstract form of justice, seeing the truth about yourself, your life, and those around you realistically and for what it is. Weigh all sides of a situation and make a fair-minded decision, even if your choice is not necessarily your first preference.

REVERSED

Is there a legal issue or legal consideration being discussed? Is someone putting pressure on you? Be careful of getting pulled into someone else's bias, prejudice, or bigotry, and don't turn a blind eye to injustice. Be aware and beware of a lack of accountability, dishonesty, or inaccuracy. Don't join in conspiracy theories or hurtful gossip, and remember that for every cause, there is an effect. Balance is crucial to your overall well-being.

THE HANGED MAN (12)

Keyword: **Perspective**

The Hanged Man hangs upside down on a T-shaped cross, bound by one foot versus his neck. He's relaxed with seemingly no physical discomfort. A halo surrounds his head, symbolizing an awareness or realization of something. His left foot is unbound, bent, and tucked under his bound foot. His arms are held behind him, perhaps a sign that someone or something is holding him back.

When the Hanged Man appears in a reading, it's a sign of being suspended in time, surrendering to someone or something, or sacrificing something for the greater good. The man looks weirdly serene for a person whose body is dangling by a rope around his foot. Hanging inverted must be painful and uncomfortable, yet he seems peaceful. How did he get into that position? What will he do now that he's in it? Perhaps he's hanging by a thread—not in bodily terms, but in a situation or a relationship. It may suggest a time in your life when you're being forced to make a decision you don't want to make. Or you may be in the middle of someone else's drama, and the only way to free yourself is to make a tough but necessary decision. The Hanged Man signifies liberation, sacrifice, independence, absolution, punishment, and release from guilt or obligation. We can think of the Hanged Man as a literal reversal of perspective. Turn the world upside down, and what do you see? New perspectives or even new solutions? In readings about conflict, problems, and disagreement, the Hanged Man instructs us to look at the issue from a different viewpoint. Accept your circumstances, allow your perspective to shift, and hang in there.

REVERSED

The Hanged Man, in reverse, is standing upright as if leaning rather than hanging. Perhaps it suggests that you are wary about someone or something or are unwilling to take the steps necessary to protect yourself. Try not to sacrifice yourself for the good of someone else. It will be a pointless sacrifice. Don't procrastinate; whatever you need to do, do it. Don't delay what needs to be done, and resist the temptation of laziness and selfishness. Though you may think your personal trials are more than you can handle, don't think like that. You can handle anything you put your mind to. Don't be bound by what someone else wants or expects from you: stay strong and be your own person.

DEATH (13)

Keyword: **Closure**

The Death card can represent grief for an actual death or the death of something, but it doesn't necessarily mean you or someone close to you is going to die, so relax. It does signal that *something* has ended or is soon to end, and you need to accept whatever it is. It could also mean that every beginning has an end and a purpose for its being. Closure is unavoidable, and the Death card reminds you to embrace it without fear. The skeletal figure is dressed in black armor, symbolizing invincibility and a reminder that endings are inevitable. His white horse suggests rebirth; the deceased person on the ground could represent someone already gone. The skeleton holds a black flag bearing a white, five-petal rose, reflecting spiritual enlightenment. The blazing sun sets on the horizon between two towers, a sign that the sun will rise again tomorrow. Remember that there will always be another day, another chance to make a change.

A young woman, a child, and a holy man appear to be blocking the skeletal figure, but, in the end, there is no stopping death. It spares no one and eventually comes for us all. In the background, a boat floats down the river, perhaps a nod to the mythological boats escorting the dead to the afterlife. This card could represent the spirit world or someone trying to reach out to you from the other side. The Death card bears the number 13; perhaps that number is significant to you. When the Death card is pulled, something in your life must die to make way for something new to come into being. This card reminds you that one door must close for another to open. You might need to put the past behind you and let something or someone go, or at least be at peace with whatever has happened. Don't be afraid to let go of the past, for in letting go, there is the promise of renewal and transformation.

REVERSED

Death, in reverse, might mean that you need to let go of unhealthy relationships or a bad habit. Or perhaps you're on the precipice of meaningful change but resisting it for some reason. Or you may not know how to make the change you need. Or maybe you're carrying trauma from your past, interfering with your ability to live your best life. If the Death card frightens you, pull a follow-up card. It might give you the clarity you need to feel better about it.

TEMPERANCE (14)

Keyword: **Moderation**

A winged angel wears a white robe with a triangle set in a square, perhaps representing that the triangle (humans) is bound by the Earth (square). The angel has one foot on the soil, representing the solid, grounded world, and one foot in the water, representing the ebb and flow of life. She pours water between two cups, symbolizing that what goes around comes around.

A winding path in the background leads to a glorious range of mountains, suggesting the beauty of life's journey and an approving nod to take the high road and stay true to one's life purpose and meaning. Above the mountains, a golden sun dominates the sky, encased in a glowing light, symbolizing clarity and the dawn of a new day.

The Temperance card signifies moderation, self-restraint, purposeful frugality, and good management. It can represent patience, a search for meaning, and quiet but powerful endurance. Temperance may also mean waiting for something painful and uncomfortable to pass.

The Temperance card encourages you to act with balance and patience when bringing disparate elements of your life together. If the Temperance card comes for you when your balance is out of whack, it's a call to action.

If the Temperance card is pulled when you are in the midst of making an important decision, consider that your options might not be polar opposites, and if there is a middle path, take it.

REVERSED

In reverse, Temperance may signify excessive behavior or a lack of balance in your life. Something seems extreme to a fault. Is someone overindulging? Have you recently walked away from someone who has been exhibiting unprincipled behavior? There may be competitive interests at play or a separation of something.

Or perhaps you need to let go of someone to save someone else—maybe even yourself. If you have been burning your candle at both ends, you need to step back and reevaluate.

THE DEVIL (15)

Keyword: **Temptation**

The Devil is not a card to take lightly, and the reversed Devil card is one of the few cards where the card in reverse is a good thing. The devil is depicted as a horned half-man half-goat, representing the contrast between good and evil, male and female, or humane versus animalistic. This card may signify that you or someone you are close to is a scapegoat. If so, who is engaging in the scapegoating? The Devil has the wings of a bat, often associated with diseases, and may be a sign to pay closer attention to the people surrounding you. His hypnotic stare is intimidating, indicating that someone might be watching or controlling you.

A naked and chained man and woman stand at the foot of the Devil. They have chains around their necks, but they're loose enough to be pulled over their heads. Do they not know this? What or whom are they chained to? Maybe they stay because they fear the Devil's wrath. The man and woman have horns on their heads and ominous-looking tails, which may indicate that the longer they stay with the Devil, the more like him they will become. They need to pull the chains off their necks and run.

This card may also suggest an addiction to something or someone, or maybe someone you know is trying to kick an addiction or a bad habit. You are tethered to some negative force larger than yourself, be it alcohol, drugs, a negative obsession, or a toxic relationship. Take care to avoid addiction in any form, for it will be your downfall. Are you feeling helpless or ashamed because you know that something or someone is harming you, but you aren't strong enough to do anything about it? That's what the Devil's work is.

REVERSED

The Devil, in reverse, means release, freedom, emancipation, and regaining control. A reversed card also warns against pettiness and weakness. Stay away from unjust or abusive situations. Don't be blinded by shiny objects. The Devil reversed may also suggest you're trapped in a lie or an issue you can't control. The power of the Devil is the belief that you have no alternatives, but you do. Once you've figured out what or who your Devil is, your job is to slip free from the chains.

THE TOWER (16)

Keyword: **Turmoil**

The Tower card depicts a scene of chaos and destruction. A looming tower is perched on the top of a rocky mountain. It seems that lightning has set the building on fire, suggesting someone has set your life on fire. Two people fearfully leap off the tower, not knowing if they will survive the fall, but they take their chances and do it anyway.

The lightning has knocked the crown off the top of the building, an omen that someone or something is trying to topple you. The Tower is an omen of earth-shattering, catastrophic change. A lightning strike tears down our walls, leaving nothing but rubble.

There's no way to stop the Tower from coming down. Perhaps you've been clinging to a job or relationship that no longer serves you. Or maybe you've been refusing to acknowledge an addiction or harmful lifestyle. Whatever the situation, you need to jump out of that tower ASAP. The pain of the jump will be well worth the resulting freedom. In other situations, the Tower is a catastrophic event that comes at you head-on. Reduce your pain by letting go.

The Tower is a problematic card and bodes possible negative things ahead. There may be a sudden change for the worse, calamity, damaged pride, turmoil, or a recent revelation about someone or something.

This card is not a good sign. It signifies misery, distress, ruin, indulgence, adversity, calamity, disgrace, and deception. Something terrible might be going on behind your back.

REVERSED

The Tower, in reverse, is one of the few cards where the reverse is a good thing: delayed catastrophe, tragedy averted, transformation. Don't fear the pain: no pain, no gain.

Even with the card in reverse, be warned that there is the possibility of oppression, tyranny, or a tyrant around you, someone cruel and unreasonable. Let's hope it's not you.

THE STAR (17)

Keyword: **Hope**

A woman pours water from two pitchers, with one foot on land and one in water. Her foot on land represents her need to be grounded. Her foot in the water symbolizes her ability to go with the flow. Her nakedness represents her vulnerability and purity under the vastness of the starry night sky. Behind her shines one large star, representing her star power, and seven smaller stars, conveying a sense of completeness. The number seven in numerology is seeing beyond the face of something and understanding the hidden truth. The two pitchers she holds represent the conscious (her right hand) and the subconscious (her left hand). The conscious mind controls our writing, speech, thoughts, and awareness. The subconscious mind controls recent memories, actions, and reactions, but only when we think of them and connect them to the unconscious mind, the repository for all memories.

She pours water into the pool while simultaneously pouring it onto the land, signifying that she is covering all her bases. The water on the dry land spreads out in five small streams, representing the five senses: sight, smell, hearing, taste, and touch. Do you have a connection with the number five? One of the five streams of water flows back into the pool, a reminder that what goes around comes around. It can also signify the calm before or after the storm.

The Star may suggest a time of recovery after a traumatic event. It can also be a card of inspiration and rebirth, perhaps in friendship or faith. The bird in the tree behind her is an ibis, a symbol of peace, love, and serenity. The ibis may also symbolize hope, change, and new beginnings. The Star signifies trust, belief, spirituality, and bright prospects.

REVERSED

The Star, in reverse, is a troublesome card and denotes despair, depression, insecurity, abandonment, arrogance, haughtiness, and lack of power.

You or someone you know has been unkind or disloyal, or perhaps you've been a victim of theft, or you're squandering away your money. Be strong, and don't lose faith. And whatever you do, don't show weakness.

THE MOON (18)

Keyword: **Caution**

We see a moon, but it's not dark outside. It sits between two towers, suggesting two sides of something. In astrology, the moon symbolizes life's cycle and truth. The biblical interpretation of the number 18 means life; in numerology, it signifies that angels protect you. Surrounding the moon is a blazing sun, as if they are either fighting against each other or acting in tandem. The Moon represents feminine introspection, while the Sun represents masculine extroversion. This card could symbolize a male-female thing.

At the bottom of the card is a body of water, representing the reservoir of subconscious memories. Beware of deception and illusion, and pay attention to your intuition. It's telling you something, so listen.

A lobster crawls out of the water, perhaps a warning of a bottom-feeder or someone using you. The lobster may also represent our worst impulses or most debilitating fears. A bright yellow path in front of the lobster might take it far away. Let's hope you control the lobster's path instead of vice versa. A wolf and a dog stand in the grass, howling at the moon, perhaps representing the wild versus tamed aspects of you or someone you love.

Look out for hidden enemies. Has anyone been making false accusations or defamatory statements about you or someone else? If so, don't make excuses for them and stay far away from this person. The Moon is also about the unconscious and repressed memory. Think of the moon's phases: some of the moon is always hidden, even during a full moon. Perhaps someone is hiding something from you, but trust that, over time, more information will be revealed to you.

REVERSED

The Moon, in reverse, represents deception, fear, darkness, misconception, confusion, and suppressed emotions: bottom line, be careful. Stay away from unstable or insecure people. If you've chosen to surround yourself with people you know aren't good for you, use caution and be warned that they will never change.

THE SUN (19)

Keyword: **Optimism**

The Sun card radiates and blazes with optimism and positivity. It shines in a gorgeous blue sky, representing beautiful days to come. In the background, four sunflowers grow tall, signifying joy and happiness—the number four symbolizes stability. In the forefront, a naked child sits on a regal white horse, symbolizing strength and purity. The child is smiling, arms outstretched, and has nothing to hide—what you see is what you get. In the light of the sun, everything is bright and radiant. Take this card to mean that isolation is bad for you, and the day-to-day struggles you may be feeling lately will turn themselves around, but you need to help things along. You need to get out more and do things that bring you joy.

When the Sun card is pulled, it tells you to take advantage of every day. Go on a trip, pamper yourself, and when you're feeling down, remember that the sun will shine again. The Sun card indicates that good things are coming and represents contentment, optimism, happiness, triumph, festivity, optimism, success, and vitality. If you're married or in a relationship, work hard to make it as loving and positive as it can be. And remember that nothing good comes easily.

It's also important to remember that the sun depicts a moment in time, not a perpetual state. Too much sun will turn a garden into a desert. Too much of anything is never good; we're meant to oscillate between modes of being. The Sun card reminds you to appreciate and see the world with a sense of wonder. Have you ever looked at something simple, and it made you smile with delight? The Sun card wants you to appreciate and bask in life's glory.

If you are going through a tough time, the Sun card wants you to know things will improve, but you need to help make that happen. You need to take a good, hard look at yourself, your life, and those around you. If there are things or people you need to walk away from, do it—and do it soon.

REVERSED

The Sun card in reverse signifies gloom, sorrow, pessimism, and self-doubt. Try to rediscover your inner child. Don't be so hard on yourself or those around you who love you. Let them in. Give them a chance.

JUDGEMENT (20)

Keyword: **Karma**

The Judgement card depicts nude figures emerging from their graves, gazing upward, their arms extended. Archangel Gabriel watches over them from above. An extensive ice cap or a tidal wave off in the distance suggests the overwhelming challenges and difficulties of avoiding judgment. The card indicates that you may be passing judgment on someone or someone is judging you. Be true to yourself and try not to judge others. Try, instead, to put yourself in their shoes. And make sure to give as much as you take. The Judgement card may also signify that you need to make wiser choices, keeping in mind that karma is the direct result of cause and effect.

The Judgement card indicates that you are at a significant turning point—evaluating your actions and the consequences of those actions. It might be time to decide what actions from others you will and won't continue to put up with and what you have learned from your journey through life so far. The Judgement card signifies introspection or a recent reckoning about something. There is a heightened awareness, a possible awakening, a reflection, or absolution from something that's been weighing heavily on you. Perhaps you recently had a change of heart or position on a matter. There is a possibility of a renewal of something, or maybe you recently experienced a positive outcome about something.

REVERSED

The Judgement card, in reverse, may suggest that someone is facing guilt, self-hate, doubt, lack of trust, or self-criticism.

Try to stop blaming yourself and self-forgive. Don't be afraid to ask for forgiveness, even if it's rebuffed, because the mere asking will give you power. Don't be so hard on yourself—or maybe you're being too hard on someone else.

The Judgement card, in reverse, warns of weakness or lack of courage about something. You may be postponing a decision, facing ongoing deliberations, or making a possible legal decision.

Whatever is going on, trust your intuition, and stop feeling so guilty about everything.

THE WORLD (21)

Keyword: **Resolution**

The World card depicts a naked woman wrapped in a purple cloth and dancing inside a large laurel wreath. Her body seems to be moving forward, although she looks to the side as if she sees something or someone. In her hands are two wands, maybe symbolizing that there are two sides to something, and she needs to choose which side she's on. The wreath is circular, a symbol of the continuous cycle of successful completion and new beginnings—a reminder that everything circles back again. That's the circle of life. Be proud of yourself and what you have accomplished.

Surrounding the wreath are four figures representing the four zodiac signs: the lion (Leo, July 23–August 22), bull (Taurus, April 20–May 20), cherub (Aquarius, January 20–February 18), and eagle (Scorpio, October 23–November 21).

The World card signifies the need for harmony, peace, completion, fulfillment, and wholeness. A trip may be in your future, or you may have recently traveled or just returned from a trip. Perhaps you or someone else will make a life move, or change living arrangements. Or maybe you need a change of pace or a change of place. If you haven't traveled for whatever reason: time, money, complacency—get traveling.

It may be challenging to hold onto the grandness of the World, which seems to slip between your fingers when held up against day-to-day reality, but don't be afraid to live life to its fullest.

REVERSED

The World, in reverse, signifies something being incomplete or missing. There are signs of inadequacy, deficiency, lack of closure, and shortcomings. If you've been avoiding something, deal with it head-on.

Live your best life. Don't sit back and wait for life to happen, and don't wait for something to get resolved. Take control of the matter that's been bothering you. Don't be stagnant; keep moving forward. Be unstoppable.

THE COURT CARDS EXPLAINED

PAGES

Pages often represent young children and teenagers. They are at the beginning of their journey and symbolize a new stage in life. Pages are seekers of knowledge and work hard to better themselves. Pages are also messengers and can often symbolize the presence of spirits who are trying to tell you something.

KNIGHTS

Knights often represent young adults between their twenties and the mid-thirties. Their journey has already begun, and they're focused on expanding their horizons. They have enough experience to know what they're doing but don't have the life experience that the Kings and Queens have; thus, they may be prone to making careless mistakes and questionable decisions.

QUEENS

Queens represent someone older and wiser—35-plus—and express feminine energy, nurturing, and caring for those they love. They are masters at setting the tone without imposing their views and use their power quietly but purposefully. They have the power of persuasion and subtly influence others without being seen as overbearing or pushy. Because of this, Queens are often viewed as more powerful than Kings because they're in control without anyone knowing it. The adage "Behind every great man, there is a great woman" is the general theme of the Queen cards.

KINGS

Kings represent mature and experienced individuals—35 and older—suggesting masculine energy or someone providing and caring for others. They're mentors who want to be in command: they manage, control, and stabilize the energy associated with their suit. Kings are adept at controlling their feelings, emotions, thoughts, and actions and are stable and focused on directing and achieving their dreams and goals.

THE MINOR ARCANA CARDS EXPLAINED

The 56 Minor Arcana cards represent life's practical side: the hardships, trials, and tribulations we all face daily.

The Minor Arcana cards contain four suits: Wands, Cups, Swords, and Pentacles.

Each suit is associated with one of the four elements—fire, water, air, and earth—and connected to specific zodiac signs.

The order of the tarot suits usually follows the Hermetic Order of the Golden Dawn:

Wands (Fire): Aries (3/21–4/19), Leo (7/23–8/22), Sagittarius (11/22–12/21)

Cups (Water): Cancer (6/21–7/22), Pisces (2/19–3/20), Scorpio (10/23–11/21)

Swords (Air): Aquarius (1/20–2/18), Gemini (5/21–6/20), Libra (9/23–10/22)

Pentacles (Earth): Capricorn (12/22–1/19), Taurus (4/20–5/20), Virgo (8/23–9/22)

Each of the 16 tarot court cards (Page, Knight, Queen, King) represents shedding old habits, beliefs, and mindsets to accept new perspectives and embrace growth.

One of the most common challenges for reading tarot cards is understanding the significance of the court cards.

Are they associated with you, others, events, personalities, or something else?

Does the Queen have to be a woman, or does the Page have to be a person under 20?

The answer is, as in life, nothing is as it seems.

Aside from the 16 court cards, there are 40 numbered cards, each containing 10 suit cards that symbolize the mundane of everyday life.

Each suit starts with the Ace and progresses up to 10, concluding with the four court cards—Page, Knight, Queen, and King—which complete the suit of 14 cards.

WANDS

Element: **Fire**

Keyword: **Action**

The zodiac signs often associated with Wands are Aries (March 21–April 19), Leo (July 23–August 22), and Sagittarius (November 22–December 21).

Generally, those who choose Wand cards have a lot of vigor, charm, warmth, and spirituality. Wands are the suit of spirit, so pay attention to the signs of someone coming through from the other side.

The suit of Wands is the suit of intuition and the metaphysical state of mind. Astrology connects it to the fire element. The suit of Wands represents the fire that burns within us: full of passion, excitement, and desire.

Fire is frightening, fierce, erratic, and has a life of its own. There are many creative ways to use fire, like cooking or crafting tools, but fire can also be deadly, destructive, and impossible to control, like a forest or house fire. Oxygen, heat, and fuel are all characteristics of fire. It is an element of masculinity, representing the desire and willpower of male energy. But too much fire can be destructive, potentially causing devastating loss or burnout.

Wands are considered an ego suit and brim with energy, resolve, spirituality, motivation, strength, and intuition. They can also symbolize creativity, achievement, status, power, and ambition. Wands cards advise you not to be afraid of a battle or a conflict and stress the need to handle confrontation head-on.

REVERSED

Wands, in reverse, may mean the opposite of energy and drive. They can suggest negative traits such as deception, selfish or narcissistic behavior, impulsiveness, lack of strategy, no purpose or direction, and laziness.

The reversed Wands can also remind us that a solid sleep routine, a regular exercise program, and health-conscious nourishment can result in sustained motivation and increased energy.

ACE OF WANDS

★

Keyword: **Motivation**

A hand coming out of a cloud grasps a wand. The card signifies creation, birth, family, invention, new beginnings, enterprise, money, fortune, or inheritance.

You may be experiencing a breakthrough in your relationship or career. Be persistent and never give up.

The Ace of Wands is associated with intuition, thought processes, and communication.

If any card says "YES! GO FOR IT," it's the Ace of Wands, suggesting a renewed spark of energy and a pure and brilliant flame. Your passion and inspiration burn brightly.

You launch yourself wholeheartedly into new endeavors with confidence and excitement. You feel like you can do anything, and with hard work, you might be able to.

REVERSED

The Ace of Wands, in reverse, warns that maybe you should put any big plans or moves on hold for a while. The reversed card can also mean sickness, decadence, ruin, punishment, or clouded joy.

Stay clear of narcissists, for one may soon deceive you. If you're in a slump, pick yourself up, and don't let anything or anyone get in the way of your dreams.

If you're struggling in your relationships, take time to nurture them. Nothing good comes without hard work.

Be careful how you allocate your money, and avoid gambling, gamblers, and any other high-risk monetary ventures.

And try not to be selfish, demanding, or stubborn. Keep in mind that a bit of kindness will go a long way.

TWO OF WANDS

Keyword: **Proactive**

A man stands high above the land, looking down over a large body of water to his left and a vast land with mountains to his right.

He holds a globe in his right hand, suggesting he controls his destiny. He holds a staff in his left hand, and a second staff stands to his right, meaning that perhaps he has set something or someone aside.

The Two of Wands signifies that the fire you hold inside energizes you, making you feel like you can take on the world. Use that energy wisely. You need to direct and channel your energy and remember that you can't do everything all at once, or you'll burn out.

The Two of Wands suggests that you may be in the early stages of a life change or facing a decision that will directly impact your future.

Whatever decision you make will likely have a positive outcome, but you first need to decide which direction to take.

REVERSED

The Two of Wands, in reverse, often means that you've been waiting for a situation or relationship to change for far too long. Stop waiting around and start taking your life into your own hands.

Do what you want to do, not what others think you should do. Forge your own path—this is the time to start living your life your way. Stop being passive and be more assertive.

If you're questioning your love life, ask yourself why. If the cons outweigh the pros, it may be time to part ways or take a break.

THREE OF WANDS

Keyword: **Strategy**

The Three of Wands depicts a man standing on the edge of a cliff, gazing over a strange sea of yellow. He watches three ships passing through the water in the far distance. Three sprouting wands, signifying personal growth, strength, and discovery, are firmly planted into the ground as the man tightly grasps one in his hand.

The Three of Wands asks you to reflect on your commitment to your plans and how you will bring them to fruition.

The Three of Wands reminds you that you can do what you think you can't. If there is something you have been wanting to do, now is the time to do it. Nothing of any value happens to those who wait around. Don't be afraid to take charge. Widen your horizons, get out of your comfort zone, embrace change, and start thinking in the long term.

Remember that true love takes time to nurture and is seldom smooth, so any recent relationships may struggle to get off the ground. This doesn't mean they don't have wings; patience may be in order. Don't try to force things. Before committing to a relationship, check that your partner is all you think they are.

If you're already in a relationship, remember that we all have to compromise from time to time; demanding your partner change to suit you can cause problems. Are you being realistic?

REVERSED

The Three of Wands, in reverse, indicates that, despite trying your best, you didn't receive the outcome you were hoping for. This could be due to your own delays or roadblocks. Despite all this, the card reminds you to keep pushing yourself with all the personal strength and fortitude you can muster. Don't be afraid to take chances.

The Three of Wands, in reverse, can also signify inaction. Now is not the time or place to stay quiet and complacent. Don't be afraid to say how you feel. It might seem easier to hide your feelings, but this would be unwise; you need to get any issues and disagreements out into the open.

FOUR OF WANDS

Keyword: Celebration

A gorgeous garland hangs across four wands planted in the ground. Could it be a chuppah, under which a couple stands during a Jewish wedding ceremony? Or perhaps you will soon be celebrating an anniversary, birthday, or other significant milestone.

Two figures are lifting flowers in the air. Beside them is an old manor house, perhaps the location of their wedding reception or other celebration.

The Four of Wands suggests tranquility, harmony, family, prosperity, and peace. It's time to celebrate and share your happiness with others. Throw a party and rejoice with your loved ones.

Expect everything worth having to take time and effort. Remember that even in love, you need to play the long game—you have only completed the first phase of many. But for now, enjoy the bounty and celebrate.

REVERSED

The Four of Wands, in reverse, still signifies beauty, happiness, and all good and peaceful things, but you'll have to work harder to achieve it.

Concentrate on your love life and give it all the attention it needs. Your relationship will be better for it.

The reversed card may also signify breaking free from a distressing situation. If you're in an unhappy relationship, get out of it. It might take some time, but if anyone can do it, you can.

Don't stay in a trapped situation or relationship. Find your happiness—it's waiting just around the corner.

Or perhaps someone is trying to ruin your celebration or stop you from celebrating. Don't let anyone dictate or cause you to question your happiness or judgment. No one should have that kind of power over you.

FIVE OF WANDS

★

Keyword: **Control**

A gang of youths are brandishing wands as if in sport or strife. It could signify a fight, strenuous competition, or a struggle of some kind. This card often indicates dominance, head game-playing, or control. The Five of Wands is generally a card of conflict or warfare. Someone may be against you, so beware.

If you're in a conflict with someone, you need to ask yourself if whatever is going on is worth the aggravation. You should also honestly ask yourself who is the stronger of the two. And never use dirty tactics to get your desired outcome unless you have no choice. But be careful with how you wield the dirt because you could lose the respect of someone very important to you.

In numerology, fives usually indicate discord. When the Five of Wands appears, it's time to end your conflicts and clear the air. Is there some discord going on in your life? Are you involved in a dispute that's been dragging on for what seems like forever? If so, it will take some time to work through, but get it resolved. It won't fix itself. If you want to improve your situation, you need to have an honest conversation with yourself before trying to resolve the issue.

There might be a battle of egos, a divorce or relationship breakup, a conflict with a child, or fighting between siblings. You may be getting into arguments, or maybe you're facing stiff competition concerning something. To succeed, you need to turn this conflict into something that strengthens you and those around you. You have to fight for what you want. In the end, it will be well worth the effort.

REVERSED

The Five of Wands, in reverse, suggests that you are avoiding the inevitable. Stop deflecting and take control of your life. Do what makes you happy, and stop worrying about what others will think. You don't have to prove yourself to anyone but yourself.

You may also be a victim of trickery, litigation, or other legal disputes. If you try to resolve the issue and are unsuccessful, know it's okay to let it go.

SIX OF WANDS

★

Keyword: Triumph

A laureled horseman bears a staff adorned with a laurel crown, perhaps a crown of hope. Footmen with wands are at his side.

On the surface, it seems as if the horseman has been victorious or is triumphing over something. It can also mean that someone will soon be bringing you fantastic news.

When the Six of Wands shows up, success at something is at hand. It could be a sense of internal satisfaction or public recognition. It seems that life is going very well for you. But it didn't come easy. Nothing ever does.

But you have achieved victory. You've survived, and you've prevailed, and you're finally getting the attention and recognition you deserve.

Enjoy the moment, but understand that your victory may be temporary. Bask in the success of your actions while they last, remembering that nothing lasts forever.

REVERSED

When the Six of Wands appears in reverse, you may still be victorious, but it may be bittersweet.

A reversed card can also signify apprehension, fear, a victorious enemy at your door, or a door unwittingly opened to an enemy or someone with bad intentions.

Beware of treachery, betrayal, or disloyalty. Someone may be talking about you behind your back or trying to blemish your reputation.

Take charge of your life, trust your intuition, and never let go of your dreams. The stronger you feel, the stronger you will become. Stand tall and stand up for yourself. And fight for what you believe in.

SEVEN OF WANDS

★

Keyword: **Confrontation**

A worried young man teeters on the edge of a rocky cliff, defending himself with one wand while six other wands are raised toward him from below. It's a card of courage and confrontation. The six wands might be attacking the young man, although it appears that, at least for now, he has the upper hand.

On an intellectual level, it may symbolize a tough negotiation, an ongoing argument, or litigation. It's a card of personal satisfaction: the young man is on top, and his enemies may be unable to reach him.

The Seven of Wands reminds us that when the going is tough, you need all the strength you can muster to achieve your goal. You may be up against someone malicious who has no intention of giving you a pass. Play by the rules, but give it everything you have. Watch out for your opponent because not everyone plays fair.

If you feel attacked, you must defend your beliefs and stand your ground. If you're being attacked, who is attacking you? Is it a person you know, a corrupt system, or maybe a former lover or frenemy?

If no one supports you and you feel alone, don't worry. Fight with conviction and hold onto your beliefs.

REVERSED

The Seven of Wands, in reverse, warns that your sense of inadequacy can cause failure in any endeavor you attempt to achieve. Self-doubt will sabotage your efforts.

Work on building up your self-worth and confidence. Otherwise, you may end up being your own worst enemy.

A reversed card may also signify discontent about something being done to you or against you, causing embarrassment, humiliation, or anxiety. Hang in there.

EIGHT OF WANDS

★

Keyword: **Progress**

Eight wands appear to be raining downward toward the ground. In the background is a clear sky, suggesting that nothing will stand in the way of the wands getting to their destination.

The wands represent rapid movement forward, literally or figuratively, which may mean something significant is about to happen.

The Eight of Wands suggests that you should look at your current life situation, whether business or familial and evaluate your progress regarding the areas you feel need improvement.

You are the only one who can effect change in your life. Don't be afraid to take on the challenge. The best thing you can do for yourself is to put your foot down, stop keeping your thoughts to yourself, and mastermind the change you desire.

Be invigorated by your courage and navigate through your issues with the confidence that, eventually, you will be seen and heard, but only if you speak out firmly yet empathetically.

REVERSED

When the Eight of Wands is reversed, some things may come to a screeching halt. Don't let stagnation and indecision hold you back. If you're incapable of moving forward, reevaluate the situation.

The Eight of Wands, in reverse, is generally associated with patience. If you're in the middle of a disagreement, take the time needed to turn things around. Breathe, think, and try to relax. Be patient; if you believe everything will be fine, it will be.

The Eight of Wands in reverse may pertain to jealousy, a quarrel, or some other dispute. The negativity you're feeling now may be legitimate, but proceed carefully, or it may doom one or more of your relationships.

NINE OF WANDS

★

Keyword: **Unease**

The wary figure leans on his wand and looks around suspiciously as if waiting for an enemy or a negative consequence. His head is bandaged, suggesting he may have engaged in a physical altercation or had an accident. Behind him are eight other erect wands, perhaps designed to keep something or someone out.

This card signifies strength in opposition. If attacked, the Nine of Wands will meet the onslaught boldly. The Nine of Wands can also indicate delay, suspension, or an adjournment of something.

Consider each wand as a roadblock. The move forward is difficult, but if anyone can do it, you can. You've overcome many obstacles before, so rest if you need to, but don't give up because you're nearly there.

It's okay to question your past actions or decisions, but don't let your second-guessing block you from moving forward. And whatever you do, don't give up.

As you stand guard and protect yourself and those you love, persistence and resilience are your watchwords.

REVERSED

The Nine of Wands, in reverse, suggests that your suspicions about someone or something may be well-founded. If you think someone is up to no good or you have doubts about something or someone, then protect yourself and those around you because you're probably right.

Or maybe you no longer have the patience to deal with a particular situation, and that's okay. Whatever has changed in your attitude toward something or someone, it might be time to move on.

A reversed card may also signify obstacles, adversity, and calamity, so keep your eyes and ears open.

TEN OF WANDS

★

Keyword: **Burden**

A man is struggling and burdened by the weight of his 10 wands. His load is heavy, but he trudges on, hoping to reach the town he sees in the distance before he collapses. It's a hefty load, but he's almost there.

If the Nine of Swords follows this card and a lawsuit is pending, a loss is reasonably certain. However, you'll probably win if the Nine of Swords comes before this card.

The Ten of Wands suggests that you're stressed, overloaded, overburdened, and carrying an enormous weight on your shoulders. Proceed cautiously, and don't bite off more than you can chew.

You may be facing an uphill battle with what you've been forced to deal with, but stay true to yourself, and you will persevere.

And don't be anyone's punching bag because that will only lead to anxiety and physical and emotional exhaustion. Stand up for yourself and put your foot down.

REVERSED

The Ten of Wands, in reverse, may indicate your burden is so overwhelming that you feel helpless.

If you struggle with anxiety, depression, or emotional trauma, or you're carrying a dark secret, reach out to someone you love and trust or seek the professional help you need to make yourself whole again. And do whatever it takes to try to let it go.

Perhaps you've taken on more than you can handle. If so, take a well-needed break and, if possible, try to lighten your load.

If you're coming out of a personal economic downturn, things are on the way up, but only if you keep tight control of your finances.

PAGE OF WANDS

Keyword: **Potential**

A young man gazes in wonder at the sprouting wand he holds in both hands. The landscape in the background is barren and mountainous, implying that growth and potential can be found in the most unlikely of places. Like all Pages, he comes with a message—good news may be coming your way. It might also mean that the truth about something will be revealed soon.

If the card before the Page of Wands is a man, he's trustworthy and reliable. If the Page of Cups follows the Page of Wands, he's a dangerous rival and should be avoided at all costs. If you have concerns about someone or something, especially if it involves deceptive behavior, tackle it head-on and get to the bottom of it. If you see something that's bothering you, speak up.

The Page of Wands encourages you to express yourself with straightforward abandon. Listen to your gut, follow your heart, and try your best to ignore the negative voices in your head. With persistence and courage, you can change the course of your future.

REVERSED

The Page of Wands, in reverse, still means news may be coming your way, but it might come from a questionable, unreliable source. Be sure to validate the information you receive as well as the person who gave it to you. Do they have more to gain by telling the truth or feeding you misinformation?

You may be in a situation where you love someone more than that person loves you. Don't grovel for their attention. It's not a good look, and you deserve so much better than that. If they don't love you, let them go. If they come back, it's a win-win for both of you. If they never come back, it's okay to mourn the loss. But remember, they've also lost you—a loss for which they may never recover.

The reversed Page of Wands can also signify indecision, instability, bad news, a negative medical report, or a rumor or detrimental story about someone—hopefully not you.

KNIGHT OF WANDS

Keyword: **Daredevil**

The Knight of Wands is in full armor and wears a yellow robe decorated with salamanders, which are associated with the element of fire. He sits on his horse, which rises up on its back legs, poised and ready for action. The Knight of Wands is armed with a short, sprouting wand in his right hand, symbolizing the growing need for action or growth regarding his life's mission. Dry, arid mountains loom in the distance, which could signify a desert or other barren land.

The Knight of Wands is on a mission to find the truth he seeks without the influence of others. This person is extremely headstrong and needs to reach their own conclusions. And yet, as hard as he tries, the Knight of Wands may never find that elusive thing he's forever searching for. He's often unable to be faithful or incapable of sticking with anything for any length of time.

He does have the uncanny ability, though, to galvanize others into action. His charm and enthusiasm are contagious, but don't expect him to stay in one place for very long. Trying to rein him in will prove useless, so don't waste your time or energy. And be warned that he's as wild as the wind and will, in all probability, continue his wild ways until his death. Speaking of death, perhaps he represents the spirit of someone long gone.

The Knight of Wands is impatient and impulsive. His modus operandi is "act first, think later." He tends to rush head-first into situations without any consideration or thought as to the ramifications of his hasty actions. He believes what he believes, and nothing you can say or do will change his mind, so don't bother.

REVERSED

The Knight of Wands, in reverse, is often temperamental and overly extreme in his actions, passions, or beliefs. He's easily frustrated; if he lashes out and hurts someone, he rarely owns his bad behavior or apologizes.

A reversed card may signify a rupture, division, interruption, or discord. If this is the case, deal with the situation head-on, move on, and never look back.

QUEEN OF WANDS

Keyword: **Strength**

Lions are everywhere, perhaps suggesting the Queen of Wands may have a connection to the astrological sign of Leo (July 23–August 22). Lions adorn her throne, a lion pin clasps her cape, and a banner of lions flanks her from behind. The lions, symbolic of fire and strength, surround her, perhaps protecting her. Sunflowers also surround her—from behind, on her crown, and in her left hand—a symbol of positivity, optimism, loyalty, and longevity. She holds a wand in her right hand, with three tiny sprouts springing to life. The number three in numerology is a symbol of confidence and self-reliance. A black cat sits at her feet as if standing guard, symbolizing spiritual protection. Perhaps a spirit is trying to come through.

Emotionally and otherwise, the Queen of Wands' personality is magnetic. Money is essential to her, but she's generous with it. She hasn't always been lucky in love and often mistrusts the opposite sex. If the card on either side of her is a man, he is someone who cares for you.

If the card on either side of her is a woman, she has a significant connection to you.

The Queen of Wands is self-confident, charismatic, and extremely kind. But don't mistake her kindness for weakness.

The Queen of Wands is an extrovert, warm, passionate, a good listener, and someone to turn to in times of difficulty. She's generous to a fault and easy to get along with. The Queen knows what she wants, knows how to get it, and is masterful at achieving her goals. She isn't afraid to express herself, her beliefs, or her passions with authenticity, truthfulness, and courage, even in the face of adversity.

REVERSED

The Queen of Wands reversed is still outgoing, social, generous, and at your service, but she may be far more manipulative, although her intentions are good.

Her interactions with others are often transactional and based on what benefit she can attain. If you can't do something for her, she might not waste her time on you. Be careful because she can be competitive and sneaky. Reversed can also signify opposition, jealousy, deceit, and infidelity.

KING OF WANDS

★

Keyword: **Influence**

Lions protect the King of Wands from behind, which may indicate that he is a Leo (July 23–August 22) or that a Leo is someone connected to him. He sits on his throne holding a blossoming wand in his hand, a symbol of life and creativity. His throne and cape are decorated with lions and salamanders, both symbols of fire and strength.

The salamanders behind him are biting their tails, representing infinity and the ongoing drive to move forward against all obstacles. He wears a dark green cap of maintenance beneath his crown, which signifies affluence and influence. He has a dominant personality, but he's also understanding, genuine, and nonjudgmental.

The King of Wands is incredibly determined, and when he sets a goal, he sticks to it. People respect him and know he will not only get things done, but he will do them well.

When the King of Wands is pulled, it might suggest that an opportunity is presenting itself to you, and it's up to you to decide whether or not to seize the moment and take on the challenge.

Take charge of the situation, control it, and choose the direction you wish to take. This is a time for confidence and a clear vision; doubting yourself or being indecisive will not work in your favor.

REVERSED

The King of Wands, in reverse, is excellent at his job but often lacks basic people skills. Interestingly, despite his lack of social skills, he's still very successful, which has nothing to do with how he interacts with others but is based solely on his intellectual merit.

He's a good man but set in his ways, strict in manner, yet surprisingly tolerant. Stick with him if you can. You deserve to be happy, but so does he.

CUPS

Element: Water

Keyword: Emotion

The zodiac signs often associated with Cups are Cancer (June 21–July 22), Pisces (February 19–March 20), and Scorpio (October 23–November 21).

Astrology connects the suit of Cups to the water element. As such, it symbolizes agility, fluidity, and the ever-flowing nature of water, which also possesses tremendous force and the ability to mold, change, and even destroy.

The emotional state is much like water; it can range from calm and gentle to robust, forceful, and even deadly. The water element symbolizes mobility, emotions, awareness, healing, and personal purification.

Water's nature is feminine and represents the hidden power that women wield. It's responsive, adaptive, cleansing, constantly flowing, and continuously changing.

Cups can also be associated with a container for holding things like secrets or problems.

The Cups suit follows the heart's long journey and represents compassion, empathy, kindness, personal development, sympathy, and wisdom in love and relationships.

When you pull Cups cards, they mostly signify affairs of the heart: love, emotions, affection, awareness, connections, intuition, dreams, and everything that falls under the emotional plane of expression and existence.

The suit of Cups represents the passion, attraction, and intimacy that come with love and affection. And there is no love without protection, commitment, devotion, tenderness, and trust.

ACE OF CUPS

Keyword: **Awakening**

In the Ace of Cups, a chalice overflows with five streams of water, signifying the five senses: touch, hearing, sight, smell, and taste. The chalice represents the vessel of our subconscious mind. The subconscious is our memory bank—it stores everything that has ever happened to us. The Ace of Cups represents our abundant emotion and intuition and is often associated with spirits or spiritual awakening.

A hand emerging from a cloud mass holds a chalice, symbolizing spiritual energy and influence. Does the W on the chalice have any significance to you? Below the hand is a body of water covered with water lilies, signifying the awakening of the human spirit. Often seen as a messenger from heaven, a dove holds a cross-marked wafer or host in its beak and descends downward to place it into the chalice.

The Ace of Cups may signify a new start, a new love, new opportunities, a new chapter, or a new inspiration. Something new is headed your way, but you need to be open to receiving whatever it is.

There is a direct line from your mind to your heart. Listen carefully, and don't be afraid to follow your heart's lead. It knows things, but use caution because the heart is not always rational. Embrace who you are and be vulnerable. Perhaps you're in love, or maybe it's self-love or the love of a family member or close friend.

REVERSED

In the Ace of Cups, reversed, water drains out of the cup, suggesting emptiness and loss. The letter on the chalice is now an M. Is this anyone you know?

The reversed Ace of Cups suggests that there is an emotional disconnect, discouragement, sadness, disappointment, or despair. Something may be blocking you from moving forward with someone you care about, be it a lover, partner, family member, or friend. Be cautious not to hurt the feelings of others, and beware of a false heart. Know when to create boundaries and know when to quit.

TWO OF CUPS

Keyword: **Partnership**

A man and woman stare lovingly into each other's eyes and seem to be pledging to one another. Behind them is a cloudless, blue sky. Far in the distance are rolling hills of lush green, a large house nestled into them. They each hold a cup—the woman holds hers with two hands, the man with one as he reaches toward her.

You can feel the sparks between them: there is a deep soul connection, and their loving union is undeniable. They are getting ready to drink together in a moment of harmony and trust.

She is wearing a laurel crown, a symbol of glory, and he is wearing a crown of red roses, symbolizing love and passion. Above their cups, a lion's head appears between two wings, signifying that the lion is their guardian spirit protecting and watching over them. Perhaps this spirit is a Leo (July 23–August 22).

The Two of Cups in your tarot reading may suggest that you're falling for someone and forming an intimate, unbreakable bond. It can also mean a truce with someone you've been fighting with.

REVERSED

The Two of Cups, in reverse, stresses the love of self. You can only love others if you first love yourself. If you don't love yourself, you'll never find true love.

Loving yourself also means caring for your needs and not sacrificing your well-being or sense of self to please others. Self-love means never settling for less than what you deserve.

The Two of Cups reversed can sometimes indicate a falling out, misunderstanding, or breakup with someone. To turn things around, try to open up about how you feel. You may not be successful, but at least the other person will know where you stand. You can't make someone love you—they need to figure it out for themselves.

Beware of false love, foolish antics, and hurtful accusations.

THREE OF CUPS

★

Keyword: **Friendship**

Three maidens in a garden celebrate with cups uplifted as if pledging to one another. The women seem to view each other with respect and admiration and are mutually participating in a joyous celebration. These women dance and toast each other in honor of their loving relationship. Close friendships are precious, so if this card appears in a reading, it's time to reach out to your squad. Your bond with your friends strengthens you together and as individuals. These friendships will sustain you in every aspect of your life. Try to take comfort in the certainty that they are there for you, and you are there for them.

The Three of Cups can signify the positive conclusion of a matter or indicate that you are healing from a recent event. Most importantly, it reminds you to appreciate and spend more time with your friends.

This card can also suggest a celebratory occasion with someone in your friend group who deserves acknowledgment and recognition. Alternatively, it could be a reminder to celebrate the friendships themselves. Friends who genuinely care about each other are worth appreciating and celebrating for no other reason.

REVERSED

Sometimes, the Three of Cups may come to you in a time of strife. If this is the case, it's time to call your friends. You will likely find the compassion and support you need when reaching out. Or it may be that you've been neglecting your friendships due to a romantic relationship or life's stress. If so, you need to reverse course. Your friends are essential to your well-being; appreciate them and nurture your relationships with them.

The reversed card may signify that you want to be left alone or you're having a conflict with one or more of your friends. Try not to isolate yourself. Nothing good will come from going it alone. The Three of Cups, in reverse, can also suggest that someone in your friend group is trying to sabotage you. Be wary of fake friends who care only for themselves.

FOUR OF CUPS

Keyword: **Depression**

A young man is seated under a tree, gazing at three cups on the grass before him. An arm emerges from a cloud, offering him another cup. The Four of Cups represents weariness, disgust, or depression. It's as if the three cups set before him are not enough. And even though he's being offered yet another cup, he's still unsatisfied. All those cups, but it's not enough. Why?

His arms are crossed over his chest, and he looks disappointed. Crossed arms indicate defensiveness, discomfort, uneasiness, shyness, or insecurity. His legs are also crossed. When someone feels anxious or defensive, they cross both arms and legs, offering them a sense of protection.

The Four of Cups suggests that now is not the time to retreat from your partnerships and friendships and go it alone. Things may seem to have lost their sparkle, and you feel apathetic and stagnant, but try not to retreat into yourself.

Confront what's causing you such pain. It's the only way you'll begin to heal. When someone reaches out to you, take their hand even if you don't want to. Try to set aside any negativity and appreciate those around you. Perhaps you don't see they want to help you because you're overwhelmed. Or maybe you feel like you have too much on your plate, and one more thing may cause you to crash and burn. The Four of Cups is telling you it's okay to say no once in a while.

REVERSED

The Four of Cups, in reverse, may suggest a withdrawal from something or someone—maybe even yourself. Be careful not to shut yourself off from your friends or family. Appreciate them, make the most of the time you have together, and consider their needs along with your own.

This may also be an excellent time to check in with your inner self. Ask yourself how you're doing, sort out your emotions, and make sure you're on the right track. Be honest with yourself. If you're dealing with something that's affecting your mental health, face it head-on and try to change it up. You may need to let go of something or someone to begin the healing process.

FIVE OF CUPS

Keyword: Loss

A man in a long black cloak looks down dejectedly at three toppled cups, symbolizing his failures and disappointments. Behind him stand two upright cups ready for his taking, a symbol of potential and new beginnings. However, he's so focused on his spilled cups that he misses the two that are there for him. It could be that he was careless with those three cups, perhaps representing the love given to him, but now spilled and gone. He seems like he has given himself over to grief and regret. Why didn't he appreciate what he had? Did he let an opportunity pass him by? Was he careless?

Perhaps he thinks it's too late, and he's so focused on what he's lost that he's incapable of appreciating what he still possesses—two cups full of potential. All he has to do is turn around and take them. It's a card of loss, but something remains. Three have been taken, but two are left. A bridge in the background leads to a home on the opposite side of the swiftly flowing water: if only he could move on from the over-turned cups, he could get on with his life. But instead of moving on, he wallows in self-pity. It's time for him to get over it, pull himself together, and move on because if he waits too long, those two upright cups behind him might not be there for him.

Try not to blame yourself for things in the past; move on from whatever negative emotions are holding you back. You may need to release the anger and disappointment to set yourself free, remembering that forgiving doesn't mean forgetting. Try to look at your life as a half-full instead of a half-empty cup. Or even better, be happy you have a cup at all. Remember that hindsight is much more straightforward than foresight, and wisdom often comes from past mistakes.

REVERSED

The Five of Cups, in reverse, suggests you may be embarrassed by some of your past actions toward others. Stop blaming yourself for your mistakes, and don't be so hard on yourself. Instead, do something about them. Maybe you need to say you're sorry to someone. If so, just do it. You can't undo the past; what's done is done. But you can change the future. The power is all yours.

SIX OF CUPS

Keyword: **Nostalgia**

Two children are in a garden, the cups overflowing with white flowers. This is a card of memories, nostalgia, and things of the past, perhaps things that have vanished. In the background, a man is walking away. Is he someone you know? What significance does he play in the part of the house and the children?

The older child offers a cup to the younger one, signifying that someone is giving and someone is receiving. Behind the two children is a glorious house, suggesting they are—or were—well taken care of.

Perhaps you're nostalgic for a time when life was simple and pure. To restore emotional balance, you retreat to your childhood memories and long for that time in your life when your joy was as pure as your innocence.

As you look back, you return to the past and almost don't recognize the person you once were, or you may feel those memories from way back will go a long way to helping you heal and feel safe again. Maybe your memories are helping you recover, but you can't dwell in the past forever.

Perhaps the card suggests that someone needs your goodwill. Or maybe you need to contact someone you haven't been in touch with for a while—someone who means a lot to you.

Maybe you should stop living in the past: use those fond memories to create something good in your present and work toward healing from whatever is causing you to look back instead of forward.

REVERSED

If your childhood was difficult, the Six of Cups, in reverse, might signify that some of your childhood issues are coming back to haunt you. Try to remember how you have grown since then. Perhaps you didn't get to have many wonders as a child, but what's stopping you now? The past has a powerful impact on us all, but to live our best life, we need to live in the present. If looking back causes you anxiety and pain, don't do it. The mind is powerful. Use it to your best advantage.

SEVEN OF CUPS

Keyword: **Consequences**

This card represents the seven deadly sins: envy, gluttony, greed, lust, pride, sloth, and wrath. The Seven of Cups has no reversed meaning because its message is dismal no matter what direction the card is in.

Seven cups overflow with ominous visions floating in a massive storm cloud. Each cup offers the man a possibility of choices. One can quickly identify danger in some cups, but others are harder to decipher.

The cup overflowing with jewelry bling appears at first glance to be desirable. But if you examine the cup closely, the form of a woman's face seems distressed, suggesting mistrust.

The cup next to her overflows with a U-shaped laurel wreath. Does the wreath signify victory, fame, or success? If so, why is there an eerie-looking skull etched on the cup? Perhaps the laurel wreath is a sign that someone needs protection.

A blue head floating in one of the cups might signify sadness or a warning not to confuse love with lust or passion.

The covered ghost-like figure with outstretched hands floating over the cup in the center of the card may suggest that someone in your life doesn't have your best interest in mind—someone who may have recently ghosted you or someone with evil intent hiding in plain sight.

Next to the ghost-like figure is a cup containing a serpent, its tongue touching the ghostly figure. Perhaps the snake has poisoned its prey, which is why the figure pulsates in red. Beware of snakes.

A castle protrudes from the cup on the lower left, possibly representing power, victory, and money. But it might also signify loneliness and isolation.

Finally, a menacing dragon sits atop the cup on the lower right, ready to attack. Dragons are mythical creatures whose supernatural forces may be used for good or evil, but this one is angry and ready to pounce.

The Seven of Cups warns that not everything is as it seems, so be careful what you wish for and choose wisely. Your actions may have negative consequences.

EIGHT OF CUPS

Keyword: **Regret**

In the Eight of Cups, a dejected-looking man walks away from eight cups in the foreground. Perhaps he's not walking away but turning his back on them—abandoning them. He's using a staff or cane to walk, so maybe he's not well. Or perhaps he's using it as a crutch, literally or figuratively. He walks away in the dead of night, maybe because he wants to go unnoticed, suggesting that he's escaping or avoiding something or someone. The way the cups line up, it seems like one is missing, a possible indication that something or someone is missing from this man. Perhaps he walks away with a feeling of loss and heartbreak. Or maybe he's purposefully walking away from his commitments and responsibilities. Or he's possibly looking for love in all the wrong places. Regardless, he walks away, his back to the cups.

It looks like his head is turned slightly to the left. Perhaps he's gauging the height of the mountains or the journey ahead of him. Why are the moon and the sun both out? Maybe day and night have converged, a sign of depression, apathy, regret, or the inability to see the light of day. He's on rocky land, unattached to the cups. How did he get there?

The water surrounding him symbolizes his emotions, and the hills represent the awareness that this will not be an easy journey, although he seems determined. He's walked away from the cups, symbolizing that he's turned his back on someone or something. Did he make the right choice? Perhaps he has taken the easy way out, even though he knows what he should do. But it seems that he is convinced there is only one way out, and as difficult as it seems, he's decided to follow his intuition and leave his past behind.

Perhaps you have been suffering in a relationship recently. If so, maybe it's time to accept, however painful, that the relationship might be beyond repair. If you're in a complicated or one-sided relationship, the Eight of Cups tells you that maybe it's time to move on and let go.

REVERSED

The Eight of Cups reversed asks, "Should you stay or leave?" Remember that walking away is much easier than staying and dealing with or resolving the situation. Another question may be, "Have you tried to improve things?" And never forget that the grass isn't always greener on the other side.

NINE OF CUPS

Keyword: Contentment

The seated man is content, satisfied, and proud. An abundance of cups sits on a towering arched table behind him. The Nine of Cups represents physical and mental wellness, contentment, victory, success, advantage, and personal satisfaction.

Perhaps your hard work has finally reaped some benefits. Your new outlook on life is to eat, drink, and be merry. You celebrate in the warm glow of your achievements, and it's your time to sit back and relax.

You can finally afford to indulge, surrounded by bounty. Lift your glass and celebrate the fruits of your labor.

The Nine of Cups may signify a hard-earned success or a positive return on a money-making venture, but most often, it's simply about gratitude and appreciation. Take a deep breath and marvel at the life you've built for yourself. Celebrate your life and find joy in the moment.

REVERSED

If you struggle to see the positive side of things, remember to count your blessings and be grateful for all you have and who you have: you have so much to be thankful for.

The Nine of Cups, in reverse, is not downbeat but uplifting and signifies truth, loyalty, and personal freedom.

However, some negatives can be associated with the reversed card, like making selfish decisions or surrounding yourself with the wrong people.

Never forget that no one is perfect—including you—so if someone has wronged you, give them another chance. You might be pleasantly surprised.

TEN OF CUPS

Keyword: **Stability**

This card is a great omen. Notice the idyllic imagery in the card: a loving couple stands together as their two happy children play nearby; the man's right arm is wrapped lovingly around her. A house in the background is high up on a hill, and a brilliant rainbow of cups dominates the sky. This couple seems to have everything—a home, kids, and a beautiful and inviting environment.

The Ten of Cups symbolizes stability and belonging. The river represents the ebb and flow of emotion, the eternity of time. The grassy hills represent good health and vitality. The rainbow symbolizes hope and faith and may signify that a spirit or spirits are watching over you.

The Ten of Cups is about family, but the definition of family is broad. Many people find family outside of the one into which they were born. Your family may be biological, chosen, or adopted. Your family could be friends, roommates, or your pet(s). This card encourages you to consider whom your family includes and to treat them with tender, loving care because you mean a lot to them.

You need to bask in the unconditional love of family—chosen, found, or otherwise. You need to embrace contentment and see the harmony around you. There will be cycles of joy and sorrow, pleasure and pain, empathy and apathy. It's okay. That's life. And for now, just for right now, there is a hand in your hand and a rainbow above you.

REVERSED

The Ten of Cups, in reverse, suggests that if things aren't going your way, then you should change them up and alter the course of your trajectory. If your life is not as stable as you think it should be, talk it out with your loved ones. Be true to yourself to ensure that your personal choices aren't misaligned.

Don't be tempted by the false illusion that there is something better for you. And whatever you do, don't sabotage what you have worked so hard to build.

PAGE OF CUPS

Keyword: **Confidence**

The Page of Cups is a message that you are on the right track and a sign of good times to come. The Page is young or young in spirit. He stands tall and confident, holds a cup in his right hand, and gazes upon the fish emerging from the cup, denoting emotion, intuition, and creativity. Fish symbols often represent life and birth. The man stands on firm ground as the water behind him flows choppily.

The Page of Cups might mean you are on the cusp of a new feeling about something or someone. This Page is a gentle soul, quiet and reflective, and cares a lot about the feelings and emotions of others.

The Page of Cups often signifies a positive message or happy news about loved ones—perhaps an engagement, marriage, birth of a child, a pregnancy, a promising business venture or plan, or a new relationship. This message is unexpected but welcomed, and you will likely respond to the news or message with optimism and hope.

Money-wise, the Page of Cups carries a positive message, but be prudent when making financial planning or investment decisions. Make sure you do your homework before investing your money.

Healthwise, the Page of Cups bears positive news, which can be a test returning the desired result or a clean bill of health.

Spiritually, the Page of Cups may indicate that a spirit may be trying to come through to you.

REVERSED

The Page of Cups, in reverse, suggests bad news, obsession, vanity, envy, jealousy, unrequited love, vindictiveness, emotional vulnerability, and heartbreak. Listen to your inner voice and avoid narcissists, attention seekers, entitled behavior, or drama queens. And stay away from players, for they will surely break your heart.

KNIGHT OF CUPS

Keyword: **Daydreamer**

The Knight of Cups is graceful and not warlike. Perhaps he is your son, brother, knight in shining armor, lover, or friend. Or maybe it's you.

He's not charging forward but rides quietly. He wears a winged helmet and armor adorned with fish, a symbol of life and birth. He holds a large cup in his right hand as if to offer it to someone, perhaps because he's generous.

In the background are trees dotting the hills and cliffs on the far side of the river, and the ground on which this Knight's horse has taken him is barren, almost desert-like, suggesting he prefers a warm, dry climate.

The Knight of Cups is romantic, dreamy, and somewhat naive. He loves to be in love and may hold an idealized vision of what love should be. His vision doesn't include diapers, baby wipes, or picking up dog poop, but if you ask him to do it, he will.

The Knight of Cups will share his feelings, although you may have to pull them out of him—but gently. He can empathize with the pain of others but often keeps his pain—emotional or physical—to himself. When faced with conflict, he frequently shies away.

The Knight of Cups is charming and romantic but not always as ambitious as he could or should be. But as with the other Knights, maturity, common sense, and business acumen will come with age.

REVERSED

The Knight of Cups, in reverse, may signify trickery, duplicity, swindling, or fraud.

Don't make hasty decisions without first thinking them through. Remember that actions speak louder than words. Don't let your emotions get the better of you; face your problems head-on.

QUEEN OF CUPS

Keyword: **Empathy**

The Queen of Cups sits on a throne beside the shore, surrounded by angels. She appears to be on an island, the water almost reaching her feet. She holds a beautiful chalice-like glass with two attached candle holders adorned with angels. Her throne is also decorated with angels, perhaps indicating that an angel spirit is trying to come through.

The Queen of Cups has many layers. She's successful, affectionate, kind, honest, intelligent, and devoted. She's also a good wife and a loving, generous mother.

Her emotions may sometimes get the best of her, but those around her appreciate the power of her warmheartedness. As a result, she's the person others call for guidance, and they open up to her in a way they don't open up to others.

She's a woman who knows when something is wrong before you even open your mouth. Her intuition is uncanny, and she has a unique talent for picking up on emotional energy, although she may suffer from depression and hide her demons from you as best she can.

REVERSED

The Queen of Cups, in reverse, suggests that you treat yourself with the same compassion and understanding that you so easily offer to others. And don't be afraid to ask for help if you need it.

Be mindful that you can only be there for those you love if you are mentally and physically healthy yourself. Know when to back off, though.

Beware of negative, co-dependent relationships. Don't be too clingy—and know when to loosen the reins.

KING OF CUPS

Keyword: **Calm**

The King of Cups is a gentle and fair man, perhaps a man of business, law, or divinity. The King of Cups sits on a throne in the middle of a turbulent sea. Far in the distance behind him is a ship. A fish-like creature is coming out of the water, and the King has a fish around his neck, representing fertility and new beginnings. The King is wise, responsible, quiet, and kind. He is the one his family and friends turn to when they need a comforting word. Think of him as a safe harbor in a storm. His greatest gift is his emotional maturity and ability to deal with life's ups and downs. He is emotionally very calm and stable and rarely loses his temper. He's the one you should go to when you need sound advice.

The King usually has few, if any, enemies, as he is well-liked and gets along with just about everyone. He's a good husband, partner, and father. He's also financially stable and secure, but he needs to work on balancing his work and home life because work often consumes him. You need to help him with that.

REVERSED

The King of Cups reversed is a bad guy: emotionally immature, uncaring, unkind, overwhelmed, anxious, gullible, depressed, dishonest, double-dealing, and a con man. The King of Cups reversed is overly sensitive, lacks a backbone, is shifty, and prone to emotional tirades. He's never accountable for his bad behavior and is emotionally unbalanced.

The reversed King of Cups may signify bitterness or unkind, uncaring, manipulative, controlling behavior, and in the extreme, hostility, cruelty, and abuse. He can be vindictive, spiteful, cold, calculating, deceitful, withdrawn, and untrustworthy. He's moody and sulky and often amuses himself by causing others pain.

The King of Cups may also represent perverted sexual behavior, violence, sexual assault, disloyalty, or cheating. If this is someone in your life, he's not safe to be around. Do yourself a favor: get rid of him and run for the hills. This man will stop at nothing to get what he wants.

SWORDS

Element: **Air**

Keyword: **Thought**

Swords are connected to thought, reason, communication, logic, and cognition.

The zodiac signs often associated with Swords are Aquarius (January 20–February 18), Gemini (May 21–June 20), and Libra (September 23–October 22).

Swords cards concern the intellectual dimension of consciousness: awareness of one's surroundings and self-awareness. The intellect and the mind can be our greatest weapon but also our greatest weakness.

Swords are also razor-sharp; they can cut through nonsense or represent the razor-sharp truth. Swords are also double-edged, representing two sides of an issue.

The Swords suit often warns us that underestimating the truth is frequently our downfall. Truth is the foundation for everything we do in life and is the root of joy, peace, morality, success, respect, and prosperity.

The suit of Swords is connected to the air element. Air is constantly moving, invisible, unseen, powerful, and quickly transformed.

Air can be a soft breeze or a fierce wind. Sometimes, it's fresh and clean; other times, it's stagnant, unbreathable, and terrifyingly deadly.

The suit of Swords can also reflect deep sorrow, strife, conflict, heartbreak, rage, stern judgments, a lack of empathy, verbal or emotional abuse, and a reminder of your strength despite enduring a tough life.

Swords cut deep, and the suit can suggest fear, sorrow, misfortune, self-doubt, insecurity, and self-deception, often exposing our worst enemy—ourselves.

ACE OF SWORDS

★

Keyword: **Clarity**

Above the mountains, a hand emerges from a dark, swirling cloud. The hand grips a large, mighty, double-edged sword with a crown at its tip decorated with laurel leaves. The Ace of Swords suggests that when making an important decision, you need to take swift action, commit to a specific path, and handle the situation confidently and decisively.

The Ace of Swords can signify the need to communicate your feelings honestly, embrace and accept the truth, and come to terms with whatever comes your way, even though it might be difficult.

It can also indicate a positive outcome concerning legal matters, legal contracts, or other documents that may benefit you or someone you love. Don't let your heart rule over your head regarding finances. Now is not the time to make financial decisions based on emotional or outside influences.

If you are in a romantic relationship, the Ace of Swords can indicate that you may be facing a challenge in your bond. Clear communication, honesty, and speaking up for yourself are crucial if you want the relationship you deserve.

REVERSED

The Ace of Swords, in reverse, can indicate that someone is experiencing confusion or memory loss. Are you or is someone you know misplacing or forgetting things? If so, a cognitive test may be in order. Healthwise, the Ace of Swords, in reverse, may indicate stress-related symptoms like migraines, anxiety, or fatigue that could negatively impact your physical well-being.

You may be having difficulty maintaining a healthy romantic relationship. The Ace of Swords, in reverse, may signify that you are friends or lovers with someone who will not benefit your life.

Or you may be in a relationship rife with deep-seated hostility, mistrust, or resentment, leading to nasty arguments and insults that, if not resolved, will ultimately destroy the connection. No matter what harm this person has caused you, try to let go of any negative feelings for the sake of your mental well-being.

TWO OF SWORDS

★

Keyword: **Choices**

A blindfolded woman dressed in a white robe is holding two swords on her shoulders; a crescent moon is behind her. She isn't sure what to do and can't see what surrounds her. Maybe she has been hoodwinked, deceived, or cheated on.

The Two of Swords may indicate that where there was once a single clear thought, there are now two opposing ideas—a possible impasse.

She holds the two swords across her chest. They are large and must be heavy, so holding them for long won't be sustainable.

She must put one or both swords down to remove the blindfold. Then, she'll need to choose her next move carefully.

The water is very close to her, but she can't see it. Perhaps it means she needs to use her intuition to make the next move because she's blinded by something or someone.

When faced with a decision, it's not always clear which way to go, especially when the outcome could go either way.

The Two of Swords represents that unsettling feeling of indecision or possibly being caught in the middle of something and not knowing how to proceed. If you're feeling conflicted, you may need more information or the perspective of others to gain clarity.

REVERSED

If you feel stuck in a situation or relationship, analyze what is causing you to feel this way. Waiting things out might be your best option at this time. Try not to make any hasty decisions, or you might regret it.

Take charge of your finances, and don't let others tell you how to spend your money.

THREE OF SWORDS

Keyword: Trauma

The Three of Swords is among the most negative cards in tarot. Three swords are piercing a heart with clouds and heavy rain behind them. A heart shot through with swords: this is how it feels to be heartbroken, as though your heart has been pierced. Love can hurt.

The Three of Swords may indicate a sorrowful, heartbreaking experience in the form of a lost relationship, an accidental death, or some other painful situation or memory. This card may also signify not just depression but deep emotional sorrow and perhaps stress, inadequate sleep, or a chronic health condition.

The Three of Swords suggests sickness, emotional pain, suffering, grief, hurt, sadness, loss, and heartbreak. Anguish pierces your heart, and your heart aches with loss and betrayal.

You carry scars, but you're tough and resilient and can handle whatever life throws at you. If you're willing to open up the lines of communication, your conflicts may be resolved; if not, discussing them might help unburden your load.

Don't be afraid to feel pain. You're strong, and your heart will mend. Never forget that you might be heartbroken, but your heart still beats strongly.

Do what you can to mend yourself. In doing so, you might successfully open up your heart or something much more powerful—your mind. And if not, at least you tried.

REVERSED

The Three of Swords, in reverse, is much the same as in the upright position, although it can indicate infidelity or betrayal.

It might be time to walk away from whoever is causing you pain. Avoid negative gossip, release your pain, and be open to optimism and forgiveness.

FOUR OF SWORDS

Keyword: **Struggle**

This card depicts an effigy of a man lying upon his tomb, possibly representing the spirit of someone. Three swords hang above him; the fourth sword lies beneath him. The stained-glass window depicts a woman and a praying child—perhaps the child is praying for him.

The Four of Swords may indicate that you should slow down: rest, relax, and breathe. Like our bodies, our minds also need rest to gain inner strength. Take the time you need to heal and rejuvenate.

You may need to reflect on a recent event, why it happened, and what to do about it. This time of quiet reflection combined with resting will help to soothe your heart and mind. And with proper self-care, your confusion and anguish will eventually dissipate, and you'll be able to get back to your old self again.

If you've been going through tough times recently, such as the trauma of a breakup, family problems, or someone departing, step back and take a break. Now is not the time to make long-term decisions.

REVERSED

The Four of Swords, in reverse, advises retreating and preparing for the next battle. If you're in the midst of a challenge, maybe it's time for a change—time to reevaluate or switch things up.

It is of utmost importance that you take a moment to recharge your energy so that you are better able to take on whatever is challenging you.

The Four of Swords, in reverse, suggests it might be a time of healing—physically or mentally. Now is not the time to put pressure on yourself or anyone else.

If you're overwhelmed, take some time out for yourself. Me time will go a long way in protecting and preserving your state of mind.

FIVE OF SWORDS

Keyword: **Conflict**

The Five of Swords depicts a man smiling slyly, picking three swords up from the ground while looking over his shoulder at two men walking away from him, most likely because he mistrusts them.

Two other swords lay on the ground as if a battle were fought. Who won and who lost? In the background is a cloudy, threatening sky, which signifies that although the conflict may be over, there might still be more to come.

The Five of Swords suggests that you are in a conflict about something, but it also reminds us to mend fences where possible and admit when we've been wrong. If there is a deep-rooted conflict in your life, do your best to resolve it. Is someone biased against you? If so, why? It might be best to stay clear of narrow-minded and negative people for a while.

You've been hurt before, but what good will it do to win by any means necessary? You want to come out on top, but as you size up your opponents, ask yourself: Is it worth it? Is it worth the risk of defeat and disgrace?

Dirty tactics and hostility can quickly turn victory into a loss, exposing you to criticism and alienation. You need to decide whether to walk away from this fight or not.

If you fight it out, you might win, but the cost will be high, and you may regret your actions. Alternatively, you may be one of the crying figures in the background, in which case, someone is about to screw you over.

REVERSED

If you've been through hell and back—now is your time to move forward and leave your past behind. Stop letting others dictate your future, and take matters into your own hands.

Deal with your relationship issues head-on. And don't be afraid to walk away. It will be painful, but you might have no other choice.

SIX OF SWORDS

Keyword: Transition

The Six of Swords shows a woman and a young child being rowed by a man across a body of water toward a nearby land. Is the man hired to take them to a better place, or is he accompanying them?

Her head is covered, and she's hunched over, suggesting sadness or loss as she moves away from something in her past. The child seeks safety and comfort and sits close to the woman as they journey to the unknown. Six swords are stuck in the boat with them, suggesting that the woman and child carry memories, trauma, or baggage from their past as they move forward.

While the water on the boat's right is turbulent, the sea ahead is tranquil, suggesting they're leaving a tumultuous situation behind them, bound for a more peaceful and supportive environment.

Perhaps the Six of Swords suggests it's time for you to move from turbulence to calm. You can carry with you all that you have learned, but try not to look back. Hopefully, your pain and strife will give way to calm and clarity—perhaps with the help of a man who can assist in what lies ahead.

The Six of Swords shows that you are transitioning. Though moving on is difficult and sometimes heartbreaking, it's essential for your mental well-being and physical health, and you will become a stronger person for it. Let go of whatever or whoever is holding you back and decide what you need to take with you and what you need to leave behind. Don't dwell on what you're losing, but focus instead on what you're gaining, and take the time to reflect on any emotional or detrimental baggage you're carrying as you move on.

REVERSED

The Six of Swords, in reverse, is much the same as upright: You need to walk away from a strained relationship, false hope, turbulent past, or any behavioral pattern that's not good for you.

Don't resist what you know needs to be done. Change is coming whether you like it or not, so be open to it. Don't let your past hold you back; embrace change and seek counseling if you need it.

SEVEN OF SWORDS

Keyword: **Mistrust**

The Seven of Swords is a card of dishonesty, theft, and manipulation. A man is depicted quickly but quietly walking away from an encampment with five swords, looking back in fear. Two swords remain stuck in the ground, and several ornate tents are in the background. Perhaps he's breaking his ties with this group. He carries five swords in his arms, and despite their razor-sharpness, he is unharmed. He leaves two swords behind, demonstrating that he does not wish to leave his companions unarmed and powerless. This gesture might represent his desire to cut ties with someone without causing them unnecessary harm. Or he might be leaving two people behind. Armed with his swords, he may be running away from something.

As he creeps away, he looks back and pauses for a moment. Is he avoiding something he ought to face head-on? Is he running for safety? Is he conflicted about leaving? Maybe it would have been better for him if he stopped to think about what he was doing and make sure that this was what he really needed to do and, more importantly, that this was the best way to handle himself. He sneaked away, but did he have to? Did he try hard enough before giving up?

The Seven of Wands suggests quarreling, slander, a failed plan, or annoyance at someone or something. If you can't connect with the man in this card, watch for sneaky behavior in others. Someone you trust may be deceiving you.

REVERSED

The Seven of Swords, in reverse, may indicate that you have moved on from lies and deception. Or it may signal that things are going to get worse before they get better. If someone has been dishonest, move forward with this person cautiously—even if they confess or apologize. If you are the dishonest one, come clean, understanding that you will need to earn back their trust.

Whoever perpetrated the deceit, the truth will come out. Stop playing the blame game and either deal with the situation or walk away. But if you choose to walk away, do it with kindness and grace and not like a thief in the night.

EIGHT OF SWORDS

★

Keyword: **Trapped**

The Eight of Swords is a symbol of entrapment. It depicts a woman bound and blindfolded. Eight swords surround her—three on the left and five on the right. A castle looms in the background, indicating it might be a place to escape.

She stands in the water—perhaps on a sand bar. Will the tide roll in and drown her? The barren land around her and the gray sky in the background may signify despair and her inability to break free.

Bound, blindfolded, surrounded by swords: how did she get there? Are others punishing her, or is it a trap of her own making? If her situation was caused by personal wrongdoing, she needs to face it and move on, recognizing that it might be difficult, but there's a way out for her.

The Eight of Swords may mean your thinking is constrained and limited—your thoughts and fears constrict you. But if you take the time, energy, and effort to free yourself, you can remove what binds and blinds you and move on. Avoid making any important decisions or life changes at this time because your judgment might be clouded.

Relationship-wise, you may feel trapped. Are you feeling smothered in a relationship or an unfulfilling or stale partnership you cannot leave? You may feel as though you have no choices, but this usually isn't the case if you look at the larger picture.

We deny ourselves possibilities when we're too scared of doing the hard work of communicating our needs and standing up for ourselves. To make changes, you're the only one who can take action. You're the one in control.

REVERSED

The Eight of Swords, in reverse, is a good omen and indicates that you have the power to change your life by freeing yourself from the past.

Take stock of your life—romantic or otherwise—and do what it takes to become happier and less anxious.

NINE OF SWORDS

★

Keyword: **Hardship**

This is not a good card. The Nine of Swords represents guilt, depression, mental anguish, failure, despair, miscarriage, deception, disappointment, divorce or other breakup. It can also signify an internal struggle and possible difficult times ahead.

The overwhelmed figure is sitting upright in bed in a white dressing gown and covers his face in shame, agony, or fear. What is it that keeps him sleepless, anxious, and regretful?

Nine swords float menacingly above him, possibly representing physical pain, psychological torment, or a nightmarish series of events.

The bed is adorned with a carving depicting a battle scene; the foe on the left looks like he has been struck down. The two figures fighting may symbolize the committing of a remorseful act. The torment of constantly reliving this metaphorical or literal battle may leave the man paranoid and wishing he could change his past actions.

Perhaps you've recently woken up from a troubled sleep and sat upright in the dark, your worries and anxieties swirling around in your head. You turn things over and over in your mind: past troubles, current problems, and grim visions of the future. You can't seem to find solutions.

Try to tell yourself that things won't seem so hopeless in the light of day. You'll find your way—you always have.

REVERSED

The Nine of Swords, in reverse, is not much different from the upright position, although it can suggest that you're slowly working through your issues. You need to change the trajectory of your life and let the demons go.

Maybe you're making things much more complicated than they need to be. Try to be more optimistic. Now might be the time to seek support and help from a professional.

TEN OF SWORDS

Keyword: Pain

Well, clearly, nothing good is happening here. The figure, shrouded in red, has been stabbed like a pincushion and doesn't seem to be getting up anytime soon. Generally, the Ten of Swords appears when we or someone we know has hit or is about to hit rock bottom. Is someone you know in deep trouble?

An ominous black sky rises above the fallen figure. Though all may seem hopeless, the dark sky is parting above the water, and golden light shines through. The faint outline of faraway mountains offers a glimmer of hope. The vast expanse of water is calm and peaceful in the face of the horrors that lie just beyond it, symbolizing how, despite everything, we need to continue carving out a better path for ourselves, our loved ones, and our future.

The Ten of Swords often represents an overly dramatic individual, someone for whom failure, no matter how big or small, is interpreted as the end of the world. For someone who likes to play the victim, one sword becomes ten.

Or the swords could represent that you feel pinned down, stuck in something, and unable to move. Perhaps someone has stabbed you in the back, not just once, but over and over again. But what are ten stabbing swords to someone who has been through what you have? It's time to pull yourself together. Gather your strength and rise up, and the swords will fall off your back, light as needles. Take a deep breath and plan your next move. Perhaps you've given in too quickly, or someone is harassing or bullying you. Remember that the power is all yours, but only if you act on it.

REVERSED

The Ten of Swords, in reverse, brings the same message: You're down but not out, although your problems aren't going away anytime soon.

Be very careful with money and your assets. Someone might be trying to take advantage of you. If someone has recently betrayed your trust, stay resilient, walk away, and never look back. The only person who can turn your situation around is you. If you need help, don't be embarrassed to reach out for it.

PAGE OF SWORDS

Keyword: **Chances**

A breeze blows through the young man's hair while 10 birds and the gathering clouds behind him fill the bright blue sky. The trees are tossing in the wind, and he has a determined, almost defiant look on his face as if he were ready to pounce at the slightest provocation.

The Page of Swords is a good communicator with an uncanny ability to offer a fresh perspective on things and a knack for thinking out of the box. He's unafraid of what's next. His ideas and thought patterns often appear scatterbrained, but listen to them anyway. You might feel the urge to roll your eyes or bring him back to reality, but don't do it—and don't underestimate him.

The Page of Swords tells you not to be afraid to take chances. Your biggest risk is not taking any risk at all.

The way the Page of Swords' brain works and how he views the world is unlike most others and worth the time it takes to listen to what he has to say. He's a great listener and a genuinely caring person. But don't cross him. And if you hurt him, you'll feel the wrath of his annoyance for quite some time. He forgives, but he doesn't forget.

The Page of Swords is like a green light saying, "You can do this. All you have to do is go for it." There will always be challenges with whatever option you choose, and not every choice will be the right one, but you need to follow your intuition and move forward.

If everything has been a little boring, a little stale, or—even worse—a little stuck, then everything is about to change. If you feel stuck in a situation or relationship, this is the time to do something about it.

REVERSED

The Page of Swords, in reverse, suggests you need to follow through on something. Remember that follow-through is about creating closure.

Be mindful of those around you, be aware of the impact you have on others, and don't make promises you can't keep. At the end of the day, all you have is your reputation and your integrity.

KNIGHT OF SWORDS

Keyword: Mission

The Knight of Swords depicts a young man dressed in war-like armor charging ahead on his powerful white horse into the midst of a battle, almost as if he is scattering his enemies.

The swift charging motion of his horse symbolizes the fierce energy that motivates both of them: the knight and his horse are ready for a fight. The knight's sword is held high, symbolizing that he's going after someone or something. Storm clouds are forming in the background, and the trees are tossing and bending in the strong winds, but he heads directly into it, unafraid of the possible danger and intent on completing his mission. There is no stopping this knight.

The horse's harness is decorated with images of birds and butterflies, indicating that a spirit may be trying to come through—maybe it's this Knight.

The Knight of Swords warns against ignoring your emotions. It might also suggest that you're in a sticky situation requiring you to gather the courage to take action. Nothing should stop you from going after what you want or what you feel is right and fair. If this card doesn't make sense, you may need this Knight's energy to speak up about something you've wanted to say to someone for quite a while. Take matters into your own hands and say your piece.

REVERSED

The reversed Knight of Swords is a sign that you need to control your behavior and own up to your actions when you hurt others. Just say sorry and move on.

The Knight of Swords, in reverse, is restless, impulsive, and almost at the point of burnout, so take good care of yourself physically and emotionally.

Beware of the Knight of Swords, in reverse, when it comes to love, for it can suggest someone is controlling, aggressive, and perhaps a bully. Don't let anyone try to convince you that they're right and you're wrong. And don't be strong-armed by others who want you to do things their way regardless of how you feel about it. The Knight of Swords, in reverse, also warns of conflict, intense arguments, and volatile disagreements. Should these fights become commonplace, it may be better for the two of you to part ways.

QUEEN OF SWORDS

Keyword: Unstoppable

The Queen's right hand firmly grasps and raises her sword vertically, resting it on the arm of her stone throne, symbolizing her resolve to find the truth in everything. Her left hand is outstretched and raised as if to face her fate. The side of her throne is adorned with an angel and three butterflies. A soaring bird above her indicates that a spirit is watching over her.

She is someone who knows a thing or two about sorrow. She may be a widow or mourning a loss. The Queen of Swords suggests that someone has survived shame, embarrassment, estrangement, unwanted virility, or separation.

The Queen of Swords might be you or someone who tremendously influences you, like a close friend, daughter, mother, or sister. She's fully accountable to herself and doesn't shy away from what hurts. She's a strong-willed woman who has been through a lot. Through tenacity and courage, she got through stuff and came out stronger but also a little sadder. Never try to mislead or deceive her, or she will wither you. She'll forgive, but she rarely forgets.

The Queen of Swords suggests that you use your head and not your heart in your decision-making and stick to your decision once it's made.

The Queen of Swords indicates that you do your homework before passing judgment and, more importantly, use facts and logic to uncover the truth. Don't let compassion or empathy distract you from the task at hand: it's crucial that you think with your head and not with your heart at this particular time. Try not to let your emotions get in the way.

REVERSED

The Queen of Swords, in reverse, warns of malice, bigotry, and deceit. Keep your eyes and ears open.

Is someone you love clouding your judgment? Be true to yourself and your beliefs, and try not to hurt others with your words. Sometimes, it's better to say nothing at all. In this case, silence is golden.

KING OF SWORDS

Keyword: **Authority**

The King of Swords sits in judgment on a throne engraved with butterflies, a sign that a spirit may be close by.

If the King of Swords looks like he's in control, that's because he is. But there is an enormous difference between being in control and being controlling.

This King is skilled at cutting through the nonsense and getting to the truth. He speaks with authority, can be trusted to make a fair and accurate judgment, and has an uncanny ability to direct the actions and thoughts of others.

His maturity allows him to see all sides of an argument, resulting in a good, honest, and unbiased leader.

If a recent situation worries you, the King of Swords suggests that you remain detached and objective: ascertain the truth and seek out the facts. Try to stay quiet and exercise tolerance for uninformed people who claim to know everything but, in truth, know nothing.

Try to use your intellect to prove your point. Education and experience are essential, but so are your day-to-day observations and intuition. Do your research before making any significant decisions or before giving your opinion to others about how they should live their lives.

REVERSED

In the reverse, the King of Swords may represent cruelty, evil intentions, perversity, barbarity, and breach of faith.

Are you or is someone else lacking sensitivity, emotional warmth, or empathy? If it's you, someone may be hurting terribly due to your lack of warmth toward them. If it's not you, be aware of those around you.

Perhaps someone is trying to manipulate you or is treating you disrespectfully. If so, you need to shut this person down quickly and decisively.

PENTACLES

Element: **Earth**

Keyword: **Sustenance**

The zodiac signs often associated with Pentacles are Capricorn (December 22–January 19), Taurus (April 20–May 20), and Virgo (August 23–September 22).

Pentacles is the last suit in tarot because it represents the final form of energy.

Each pentacle is a five-pointed star connected to fire, water, earth, air, and spirit. Spirits are an integral part of the suit of Pentacles.

Astrology connects Pentacles to the earth element. Primal, grounded, and fertile, the earth is the slowest-moving element and is the foundation on which everything else is built.

The suit of Pentacles represents prosperity, stability, fertility, physical and mental health, security, safety, charity, and character-building.

The suit also encompasses the material aspects of life, such as prosperity, employment, commerce, property, and wealth, representing your physical and financial well-being, career, and life endeavors.

It also stresses the importance of being grounded in the material and physical world while balancing our obligations against our pleasures.

The Pentacles suit often weaves earth and nature with building a fulfilling life by stressing the importance of putting down roots for your family, nurturing relationships, and tending to your body.

Additionally, Pentacles directly connects to self-esteem, sense of self, and ego.

This suit reflects the themes of work, money, home, environment, and family—the building blocks of life.

ACE OF PENTACLES

Keyword: **Evaluate**

A hand emerges from a cloud holding a pentacle. Below the hand is a lush garden with a path leading to an archway through which there is a mountain. The Ace of Pentacles suggests that it might be a good time for you or someone you love to seek advice from others before making any hasty monetary decisions. It may also not be the best time to jump into a new job, business opportunity, or other financial venture.

Love-wise, the Ace of Pentacles suggests that a relationship that once gave you a sense of pride and stability is now making you feel anxious and vulnerable. Be wary of people who are selfish, greedy, or willing to take advantage of you. The Ace of Pentacles may also signal missed romantic opportunities.

Concerns about finances may creep into your relationship, which may cause resentment. Sometimes, an honest discussion and a game plan for moving forward can go a long way to fixing things. The material or practical worries you're dealing with may be temporary and can be solved with careful budgeting. Do you feel like you've missed some financial opportunities along the way? If you're self-doubting yourself, you need to give yourself a break. There will always be someone out there who has more than you.

You may feel you haven't spent your recent time wisely and have made some questionable decisions over the years. It's not over until it's over. It's never too late to do anything you put your mind to. Think less about what you need to do and more about what you want to do.

REVERSED

The Ace of Pentacles, in reverse, may mean you or someone you love is facing challenging financial times. This reversed card advises you against taking significant financial risks anytime soon and to analyze your business dealings carefully, including any monetary documents, contracts, or leases.

In reverse, it may also suggest that you or your partner isn't giving your relationship the time and attention it needs to flourish and succeed.

TWO OF PENTACLES

Keyword: **Analyze**

The Two of Pentacles signifies life's ups and downs. The young man is dancing and juggling two pentacles, one in each hand. Despite all the chaos surrounding him, he's happy, seemingly living a carefree, productive life. An infinity sign connects the Pentacles in the card, representing limitless energy.

In the background, two ships are riding rough, giant waves. The water is terrifyingly choppy, but the ships are still afloat.

The balancing act depicted in this card suggests that you may be juggling two significant issues. It might be time to step back and analyze how to handle those issues more effectively. Perhaps you've taken on too much. Multi-tasking is sometimes not as time-efficient as you think. Concentrate on the two issues you believe need your attention the most, and cut back on everything else until they're resolved.

The Two of Pentacles is about duality, tough decisions, juggling more than you can handle, or holding two opposite viewpoints simultaneously, and not knowing which to choose.

Even if you struggle to keep it all together, the Two of Pentacles suggests you've got this. This is a time to be adaptable and handle your many challenges wisely and efficiently. But you need to do your best to tackle them head-on.

REVERSED

The Two of Pentacles, in reverse, is still about balance and suggests that you are anxious about the lack of balance in your life. If you're unhappy with your work-life balance, perhaps it's time to reevaluate. What metaphorical pentacles can you set aside for a while? Do whatever it takes to restore balance in your life. The key here is carving out some time for what's important to you.

Perhaps your recent decisions haven't been well thought out. You need to measure the worth of your time using your heart as well as your brain. One without the other will make for a ruinous decision. Beware of overcommitting yourself. In trying to be all things to all people, you may burn out, which helps no one, especially you.

THREE OF PENTACLES

Keyword: **Direction**

The Three of Pentacles depicts three figures—two men and a woman—seemingly working together. This card is about teamwork.

The man standing on the bench seems to be in control. The woman is holding a paper, perhaps a plan, a will, or other important document.

The Three of Pentacles suggests you might need an outside perspective on something. Don't hesitate to contact a mentor, friend, or intermediary for their advice and expertise.

Relationship-wise, the key to a loving, healthy, mutually respectful relationship is working together as a team. There is no "me" in "we."

The Three of Pentacles is often considered a "planning" card. Perhaps it's telling you to plan the work and then work the plan.

And while this may be your time to shine, the Three of Pentacles urges you to work with others to achieve the most successful outcome. Working as a team will likely provide the best possible result. In this case, three heads are better than one.

REVERSED

The Three of Pentacles, in reverse, is not much different than the upright card. It warns that even though you're tired of waiting for others to act and believe your best option is to go it alone and finish the task yourself, don't do it. Be open to asking for help, whether through assistance from others or advice.

The Three of Pentacles, in reverse, can also signify the negative side of three, such as a love triangle, a child causing a rift between two parents, or two friends pushing a third friend out. If you're in the middle of something or someone, try to maneuver yourself out.

If you're confused about the message of this card, pull another one.

Four of Pentacles

Keyword: Oblivious

The Four of Pentacles depicts a man holding on firmly to his pentacles, determined that no one is going to take them away from him. A cosmopolitan city is in the background, but he doesn't see or care about it. He's so obsessed and absorbed with his pentacles that he's immovable and incapable of enjoying what life has to offer him. He's completely oblivious, unconcerned, and could care less about anything other than his pentacles.

The Four of Pentacles suggests that you loosen your hold on whatever it is you're not willing to part with and enjoy your life. If you're able, use your resources to help others enjoy their lives as well.

You assess your money and everything else you've accumulated and hold it close. It's all yours. You earned it. You've worked hard for what you have and what you've built, but try to avoid keeping it all for yourself. You can't take it with you, so share it with others while you're still here and appreciate the joy of giving. And—as important—you need to appreciate the joy of living.

As you clutch your pentacles, you need to ask yourself: Is this prudent? Am I so focused on protecting what I have that I've missed the things worth stopping for? Try not to be so obsessed with what you have that you're oblivious to what and who is around you. Remember that you're an empty shell without the people you love. And never forget that you get what you give.

The Four of Pentacles also suggests that you may soon be involved in receiving or giving a monetary gift or inheritance.

Reversed

The Four of Pentacles, in reverse, warns against being overly protective of the people you love. You need to give them space: stop smothering them and let them live their own lives. There is such a thing as giving too much. You want to help, but you don't want to render your loved ones unable to help themselves.

Your spending habits may soon exceed your earnings, so try to live within your means.

FIVE OF PENTACLES

Keyword: **Adversity**

This card shows a man and a woman, down on their luck, struggling through harsh, snowy weather. The man is afflicted, one leg in a boot or cast, and carries a cane. Behind them, a church window is glowing with light. The church symbolizes a safe place where they can rest and warm up. If they go into the church, they might make it through the night. But it seems that they don't see the church. Will they notice this safe place, or are they too stuck in their pain to see it? If they see it, will they choose to accept help or choose to suffer instead?

Do you feel like you've lost something or someone? Have you encountered a tough time or a difficult situation? You might be at a crossroads, unable to take care of yourself or others, and as a result, you've closed yourself off from the people around you. Remember that everyone has their fair share of obstacles.

You pass by those with plenty, finding yourself on the outside looking in. Would they help you if you asked? Maybe. Maybe not. But you won't know if you don't ask. Nothing good will come from trying to move forward alone.

Take the time to nurture relationships, and don't close yourself off. Remember that loneliness has no upside. You're only alone if you choose to be.

Are you in denial about a relationship or afraid to leave a toxic partnership? If so, it's time to make a change. There are people who love you and will offer you support. Whatever your cold, dark night is, seek warmth and assistance. Accept help. Whatever you do, don't be afraid to reach out to your loved ones.

REVERSED

The Five of Pentacles, in reverse, may indicate a family rift or problems in one or more of your relationships. It may also be a sign that you need to walk away from the toxic people in your life. Keep your eye out for someone who might try to deceive or undermine you. Additionally, the Five of Pentacles, in reverse, can indicate a health problem, marital trouble, familial or monetary ruin, chaos, disorder, or discord.

SIX OF PENTACLES

★

Keyword: **Generosity**

The Six of Pentacles depicts a man dressed in a red robe doling out coins to two figures who kneel beside him. He holds a balance scale in his left hand, representing fairness and equality. The figure on the left is getting more than the figure on the right, which suggests that you take another look at both sides of something, or perhaps there are two people in your life, and one is getting more than the other.

The Six of Pentacles is a card of haves and have-nots but can also suggest generosity. It indicates that you should share your wealth and abundance with others if you have the means. It also speaks to accepting generosity and letting others assist you sometimes.

The Six of Pentacles reminds us that giving is as important as receiving. Sometimes, you're on the receiving end; other times, you're on the giving end.

It's an ongoing life cycle, and the balance scale reminds us that, in most cases, nothing is equal. The balance of things can change at any moment. You may have all that you need today, but the time may come when you need the support and help of others. By showing generosity and support toward others, they'll be more inclined to repay you in kind.

You know what it means to be generous and the importance of material and spiritual balance. Perhaps someone helped you when you were struggling and shared what they had. As a result, you learned the value of give and take. Or maybe you came from nothing, so you feel compelled to help others. When someone you love needs assistance, open your arms to them.

REVERSED

The Six of Pentacles, in reverse, warns of the danger of someone abusing your generosity. Be careful that you don't get taken advantage of. And beware of gifts with strings attached to them. Whatever you do, don't try to control someone with money. This will only weaken, not strengthen, their character.

And try not to get stuck in the past. Nothing good will come from that, either. Let the past go.

SEVEN OF PENTACLES

★

Keyword: **Reflection**

A young man is leaning on a garden hoe, gazing satisfactorily at his abundant crop adorned with six pentacles. The seventh pentacle is at his feet.

Metaphorically speaking, perhaps you have laid the groundwork for something, and your efforts are beginning to bear fruit. Enjoy the fruits of your labor, but take time to step back and assess your progress—the work you've done and the work you have yet to do.

The Seven of Pentacles is about reflecting upon your life, but it is also a card of money, business, and barter.

The Seven of Pentacles suggests that you need to be clever, perceptive, and resourceful.

It's time to reflect on what you've built and ask yourself if you're still on the right path. If, for some reason, you're off track, you need to figure out why.

Relationship-wise, don't be frustrated by slow and steady. By taking things slowly, you can build a true and lasting connection. It all comes down to two things: relationships going somewhere—or relationships going nowhere. Either way, only time will tell, so take all the time you need to see if your relationship has what it takes to go the distance.

REVERSED

The Seven of Pentacles, in reverse, may signify some anxiety about money, a quarrel, or some other altercation.

You might be disappointed that all your efforts have yielded nothing of substance. Don't despair, and don't give up. Nothing comes easily. Keep at it, but know when to walk away.

If you're having a rough patch in a relationship, you may need to take a break, step back, and reassess. But if this relationship is essential to you, do what needs to be done to make it work. Stop procrastinating and do what you know in your heart needs to be done.

EIGHT OF PENTACLES

Keyword: Diligence

A man labors intently, carefully etching out a pentacle shape into eight coins. A small town is in the background, but this man focuses entirely on his task. Perhaps he's a workaholic? Or maybe he's under enormous pressure to make as much money as possible.

The Eight of Pentacles suggests that while focusing on the intricate details of your work life is okay, balancing work and free time is as important as the daily grind.

Whatever you've been focused on recently, continue your efforts. Every day, you will learn more, and as a result, with purposeful diligence, your life will improve.

Your diligence and hard work are their own reward, but if you combine your pride and expertise in your craft with a rich and nurturing personal life, you will be happier for it and reap the rewards of both.

Whether you're the primary breadwinner or earn less than your partner, or vice versa, transparency about your perspective on your joint finances is crucial to a long-lasting relationship.

REVERSED

The Eight of Pentacles, in reverse, signifies a lack of ambition, vanity, selfishness, and narcissistic behavior.

Your lack of commitment may be your undoing. Think carefully before you walk away. Your unfinished business could be your biggest regret.

And don't be too pushy. Understand that pushiness is usually rooted in a need for control or the fear of not having a voice. You can voice your feelings at home and work without being demanding, bossy, or overbearing.

Be careful not to get roped into any business deals where you have to pay a high-interest rate or invest money you can't afford to lose into a risky venture.

NINE OF PENTACLES

Keyword: Pride

The Nine of Pentacles often connects to Taurus (April 20–May 20).

This regal-looking woman seems to have everything: a lush garden, regal clothing, a beautiful home, and a sprawling property in the distance. She's living her best life. But is she doing it alone?

Nine pentacles surround this woman. In numerology, nine is often associated with spirits and spiritual enlightenment. She gazes upon a bird with a large red crest on its head, perhaps a red-crested cardinal symbolizing courage, leadership, protection, and guardian of the home. Cardinals are also a sign that a loved one who has passed is near, letting you know they're with you. Since she gazes at this bird so lovingly, it's worth asking yourself what or whom this bird represents.

The Nine of Pentacles suggests that you are confident and proud of your achievements. You're happy and have accomplished much, but don't forget to nurture your relationships. Remember that pride can be healthy and liberating when used to build yourself up. However, pride becomes problematic when you use it to cover up your true feelings or your authentic self.

REVERSED

The Nine of Pentacles, in reverse, suggests that you seem to have everything, and yet something is missing. You may fear that you're losing your independence or your ability to speak up about what's on your mind.

Money-wise, sometimes it's okay to aim for less. Permit yourself to worry less about money and more about living. Money is necessary, but it isn't everything. Success is more than money in the bank. Your emotional wealth is as important—if not more important—than your monetary holdings.

Don't be afraid to be vulnerable in love, but be careful not to be financially used. If you feel someone is using you for your money, walk away. And whatever you do, don't be jealous or overly clingy—nobody likes that.

TEN OF PENTACLES

Keyword: **Permanence**

In the Ten of Pentacles, an older man is seated in an archway leading to a grand estate. He appears to be the patriarch, surrounded by his multi-generational family and his dogs. He wears a robe adorned with grapevines and crescent moons, indicating the joining of nature and spirit. Or perhaps he is the spirit.

The number 10 may indicate that a chapter has been completed—the end of something or a cycle coming to a close—a resolution of some kind.

The older man sits quietly, observing his family. They are vitally important to him, and he derives satisfaction from knowing they're all together. He's pleased with his accomplishments and takes pleasure from their happiness. As he watches his loved ones, he knows that his legacy will span for generations to come. He basks in the knowledge that his legacy is solid. He is relieved that, although his life is closer to the end than the beginning, he has provided well and achieved everything he set out to do.

The Ten of Pentacles suggests that all the effort and hard work you put into your life and family will pay off, and everything will work out in the end. It also implores you to make decisions that will have positive results not only in the present but also in the long term. There could be a financial or familial blessing on the way.

If you're in a relationship, the Ten of Pentacles can signify that you're lucky in love. From both emotional and material standpoints, you are a solid couple. While your relationship isn't perfect—no relationship is—you have an unbreakable bond.

REVERSED

The Ten of Pentacles, in reverse, may signify that you've hit a rough patch in a relationship, be it a marriage, romantic partner, friend, or family member. Don't be so quick to give up, and try to resolve your issues. But always remember that you can't force someone to love and respect you.

For single people, it may indicate that one or more of their relationships have been great in the short term, but they lack the substance for a lifelong commitment.

PAGE OF PENTACLES

Keyword: **Opportunity**

Pentacles in tarot are associated with the earth, our daily interactions, and our physical and material needs. Every Page card carries a message, so think about what this card might be trying to convey.

The Page of Pentacles depicts a young man standing tall in a lush, grassy field full of blooming flowers. In the far distance is a patch of trees and a meticulously plowed field, perhaps indicating an abundant yield to come. The mountain range behind the field signifies the provision of material resources and physical sustenance. He holds a gold coin with two hands, gazing at it adoringly, representing his goals and aspirations.

Stay focused on the practical and tangible, and keep your feet firmly planted on the ground. Don't get carried away with pie-in-the-sky dreams; focus on what is realistic and achievable. Your common sense and practical, pragmatic approach to issues will be the key to turning your dreams into reality.

The Page of Pentacles suggests that implementing well-thought-out plans and actions will help you achieve your dreams and long-term goals.

The Page of Pentacles has an endless thirst for knowledge and experience. He has an open, loyal personality and makes a great friend. He wants to be useful and finds great satisfaction in helping others.

REVERSED

The Page of Pentacles, in reverse, can signify a lack of progress or procrastination.

It's okay to fail sometimes. It will help you to learn from your mistakes. Nothing is going to be as perfect as you want it to be.

If you're exploring a new business or other venture, don't move on it just yet. Step away from the situation and analyze whether the benefits outweigh your time, effort, and money.

If you're in a stagnant relationship, don't be complacent: do something to improve it or break it off.

KNIGHT OF PENTACLES

Keyword: **Achievement**

The Knight of Pentacles is sometimes linked to the zodiac sign of Virgo (August 23–September 22).

The Knight of Pentacles sits on a horse, contemplating his next move, holding a coin or pentacle in his right hand.

He's dressed for battle, but his horse is stationary, suggesting the importance of patience and caution when making significant decisions.

He loves deeply but is quiet about his feelings and prefers to take things slowly. He's reliable, focused, hard-working, grounded, patient, trustworthy, and a good provider.

The Knight of Pentacles can also signify a man who is not a romantic interest but someone who will give you solid, truthful advice—someone who's not afraid to tell you like it is—and someone who won't sugarcoat your situation. If you know who this person is, take advantage of their knowledge and honest opinion.

The Knight of Pentacles is seriously underrated. He's loyal, capable of keeping a secret, and in his relationships for the long haul. He's one of the good guys.

REVERSED

In reverse, the Knight of Pentacles can be so much more than what or who he is, but for some reason, he doesn't care or doesn't know how to be his best self. Or maybe he doesn't want the pressure of being someone's person.

Try your best to nurture your relationship, but know when to walk away. His flip-flopping will only cause you pain and disappointment. He may love his autonomy and freedom more than he loves you.

The Knight of Pentacles is on a black horse, which could symbolize danger, fear, or uncertainty. Be wary of someone secretive or deceptive about money.

If this card doesn't make sense, pull another one to see who this person might be.

QUEEN OF PENTACLES

Keyword: **Family**

A dark-haired woman is seated on a magnificent throne and holds a single gold coin with both hands as if to protect and nurture her prosperity and financial achievement. A lush floral garden surrounds her, and a canopy of flowers is above her, symbolizing her respect for Mother Nature. Her throne is embellished with wild animals, connecting her to the natural world and its bounty. A powerful spirit animal—a rabbit—appears at the bottom right-hand side of the card. Perhaps a spirit is trying to tell you something.

The Queen of Pentacles is kind, loyal, and tuned into the world around her. This Queen shows her love in many ways: she cooks, cleans, and is the matriarch of her house. She also brings in a decent income to help support her family. She has created a warm and secure environment for her loved ones and would do anything for them—even when it isn't in her best interest. She's a multi-tasker—able to care for her children or animals, work a full-time job, keep an immaculate home, and still have time for her many hobbies.

The Queen of Pentacles suggests the importance of being financially independent, with a stable income, while allowing enough time and energy for family and loved ones. The Queen of Pentacles is the most down-to-earth personality in the tarot court cards. Family-oriented and home-loving, she can also make quite an impression career-wise as she is adept at juggling all aspects of her life. She's as happy baking cakes as she is bringing home the bacon. If the Queen of Pentacles is someone in your life, she's likely someone incredibly nurturing. She's practical, reliable, a great friend, and a dedicated family member. If she has come into your life, consider yourself very lucky and cherish her, for she will not fail you.

REVERSED

Stop comparing yourself to others, and be content with your life and your lot. Your stability is vital for those around you who look to you for their grounding energy. Don't disappoint them; most importantly, don't disappoint yourself. Don't let any issues or obstacles you're facing overwhelm you. You can handle them—you've done it so many times before. Don't give up now.

KING OF PENTACLES

Keyword: **Provider**

The King of Pentacles sits on a throne adorned with vines and bull carvings. His robe is embroidered with grapevines, which have been used for centuries as a symbol for providing us with the fruit of the spirit and life itself.

You can rely on this person. The King of Pentacles represents security, ambition, stability, and trustworthiness. He's a paternal figure who cares for his family by providing advice, guidance, wisdom, financial support, and wealth.

He's a provider and protector and generates much of his self-worth from what he has accumulated and what he can share with his family. He's responsible and reliable, making for a great partner, parent, and provider who freely offers both material and emotional comfort. He demonstrates his love through action instead of words and works diligently to build a financially stable and prosperous life for his family.

If you meet this person, they may be slow to commit, but that is only because they take love very seriously and need to truly understand and trust you before taking any next steps.

The King of Pentacles is a sign that your relationship is secure and solid, although nothing is without its challenges. Consider yourself lucky in love—handle your relationship with tender, loving care—and appreciate and nurture it.

REVERSED

The King of Pentacles, in reverse, warns of money problems—so watch your spending. It can also signify bankruptcy or being cut out of something, maybe a will.

The reversed card may also indicate someone who is stingy, greedy, stubborn, materialistic, and possessive, whose negative traits hold him back and make him a lousy love choice. And never forget that you can't change people.

Take care not to lose yourself. If you feel stagnant or unhappy in your life, do something about it. Life is short—enjoy it while you can.

ABOUT THE AUTHOR

Teri Schure is the founder of the international news website *Worldpress.org*, a freelance journalist, writer, blogger, and business consultant.

Her blog, *The Teri Tome*, attracts over 30,000 page views per month, plus an additional 50,000 on *Worldpress.org*.

Teri has been an executive director at *Newsweek*, a publisher and COO of *World Press Review* magazine, and in 2007, was *Commentary* magazine's first female publisher since its founding in 1945.

Her first novel, *Our Romantic Getaway*, was published in 2014, followed by a children's book, *The Day It Snowed Popcorn*, in 2019.

For more information about Teri, her life's storms, frailties, shortcomings, and random musings, go to her blog at blog.terischure.com or her author website at terischure.com.

www.ingramcontent.com/pod-product-compliance
Lightning Source LLC
Chambersburg PA
CBHW082211070526
44585CB00020B/2375